HAPPINESS RULES

HAPPINESS RULES

✓ **BEAT BURNOUT**

✓ **EMBRACE HAPPINESS**

✓ **BECOME A BETTER ENTREPRENEUR**

MANUEL ASTRUC, MD

LIONCREST
PUBLISHING

HAPPINESS RULES
Beat Burnout, Embrace Happiness, and Become a Better Entrepreneur

FIRST EDITION

ISBN   978-1-5445-3627-9   *Hardcover*
      978-1-5445-3628-6   *Paperback*
      978-1-5445-3629-3   *Ebook*

FOR MY TWIN

CONTENTS

INTRODUCTION

"When we are no longer able to change a situation...we are challenged to change ourselves."

—VIKTOR FRANKL, *MAN'S SEARCH FOR MEANING*

In September 2008, I hit rock bottom. This wasn't my first time falling so low—I'd also spent time down there when facing alcoholism and depression—however, I'd never felt *this* exhausted, desperate, and bitter. As far as I could tell, life was intolerably difficult, and it was never going to get better. I had financial commitments I felt I could never meet; I was worn out and couldn't take a break; I was struggling to keep afloat; and I saw no way out of my predicament. In that moment, I saw no potential for a better future, let alone relief from my suffering. My situation felt so hopeless, I even contemplated suicide.

It wasn't drugs or alcohol that led to this moment of despair; it was, in a way, success. I had worked myself so hard and provided myself with so few resources to recover that life had simply become too much for me. I was suffering from burnout, and I didn't see any way out of it.

Because I had put everything into my work, I had isolated myself from those who cared for me. My second wife and I were separated. My relationships with my kids—all six of them—were strained. I saw no way to amend my behavior and repair any of those relationships. Quite the opposite, in fact. All I could see in those relationships at the time were obligations that trapped me in a cycle of overworking. I carried with me from childhood a deep conviction that my role must be the provider, fulfilling all my family's financial needs. Six kids and two ex-wives led to a lot of bills. I had alimony and child support to pay. My older children were heading to college, and I'd either have to find the funds to cover their education or face the humiliation of letting them down when they needed me most. And that was before I spent a cent on myself.

The only solution I could imagine was to work more. After all, that had always been my solution to everything. I was a hard worker by nature, and I'd built up a very successful psychiatric practice through that industriousness. It was a point of pride for me that I could outwork anybody. For years, I'd regularly put in fourteen-hour days at the office, six days a week. But how many more hours could I realistically work? And what was I going to do now that I could barely get out of bed to go to the office, let alone put in a long shift?

I simply couldn't step back from my responsibilities. Not only did I have huge bills to pay, my work was important. I had responsibilities to my patients. I couldn't justify days off or ducking out of the office early. Who else could handle my responsibilities? Who would sit in those therapy sessions or write prescriptions? If I turned my attention away, the whole practice could crumble.

In my despair, I could still recognize the irony of my situation. I'd turned off every other aspect of my life, and now the one thing I put everything into, the one thing I felt I could do as well as anyone in the world—my work—was draining me of my final remaining resources and leaving me feeling weary and resigned. Worse, I'd seen this coming for years. I knew eventually there would be a day of reckoning. But I'd been so worn into the grooves of my workaholism, I'd slammed right into the wall I knew was just around the corner. Because of that failure to change course, I now felt stuck going through the motions, no matter how exhausted I became. Where once my work had invigorated me, it now felt like an endless trudge on a treadmill. And I could feel my legs giving out under me.

Like an exhausted runner, I could no longer keep up my stride. I was slipping. Because I was so burned out, I began to fear that I would lose the ability to work at the highest level of psychiatry. Instead of providing insight into the lives of my patients, my lack of focus left me less sharp. When I did focus, it was always the small number of patients who weren't getting better as fast as I wanted.

How long until my pessimism affected the treatment I offered my patients? How long could I keep this up with no end in sight?

I was trapped. I needed rest, but I needed money. Because I needed money, I had to work. If I kept working, I knew I would eventually hit a breaking point and face even more severe consequences. But what choice did I have left? As far as I could tell, all I could do was work as hard as I could for as long as I could and hope my health held out long enough for my kids to grow up and take care of themselves.

In that moment, I had to almost marvel at the cruel twist my life had taken. I had overcome depression and alcoholism only to see my darkest moment brought on by what I did best: working hard and succeeding at it.

FEELING THE BURN

This is what burnout—truly burning out—looks like. Burnout is defined by the World Health Organization as an occupational syndrome, a response to a life that is out of order. It manifests in those who constantly and consistently put work before everything else. And it causes intense disruption to your life, your work, and your health.

Burnout isn't just a sense of tiredness or a lack of enjoyment in your work. It's a dark room that feels like it has no exits. From once being the hardest worker in the office, you can feel your effort slipping away during even the most important projects. From being the most creative or decisive thinker on your team, you can feel like there are no solutions left. From being the person to get things done, you can feel like the bottleneck holding progress back. From being an innovator and trailblazer, you can feel like you are a slave to your responsibilities. From having the golden touch, you can feel like you've lost your touch completely.

But this doesn't describe *you*, right? Of course not. You're too driven, too successful, too critical to your business to ever suffer from burnout, right? Burnout is a weakness. It happens to other people, not world-beating entrepreneurs who have everything going their way. Sure, you feel so tired that lying in bed has become the best part of your day, and you feel like there is no way to change that. And sure, your once indomitable enthusiasm for your work and your life has begun to curdle into cynicism and bitterness. But this is all just part of what you have to do to play at this level, right?

...Right?

That's what we entrepreneurs tell ourselves. We assume burnout is reserved for people who truly lack options—those who are stuck in positions that don't offer any financial or personal freedom. It's for those with tough, no-excuse bosses, not the boss themselves. It's for employees who never have the option to do something else, not the well-off business owner who could find alternative employment with the snap of a finger.

We want to believe that burnout doesn't happen to people like us. It seems almost pathetic to complain about stress and melancholy when we get to make all the critical choices for our company, set our own rules and our own schedules, and pursue our dreams.

Yet for all the perks that come with entrepreneurship, our circumstances do not make us exempt from burnout, but candidates for it. In fact, as entrepreneurs, our roles check all four boxes for the pressures that push a person into burnout:

- Highly demanding work
- A low level of perceived control
- High risk associated with the job

- And a low level of perceived reward

Anyone can—and many do—face these pressures, but entrepreneurs are lucky enough to face them all constantly.

There's no doubt that your work is highly demanding and that the consequences for doing your job poorly are significant. The problems you face are never easy to solve, and if you don't solve those problems, the cost is high. You might lose major clients or have to let employees go. At worst, the whole business might come crashing down.

And once you do overcome those problems, your reward for success is bigger problems. You get bigger clients, more employees, and a larger enterprise that could all fall apart.

Check, check, and check.

But wait. How can an entrepreneur who runs their own business lack control or feel like they aren't being rewarded? Surely if anyone has control over their work, it's entrepreneurs. And isn't the big paycheck and the name on the door of the biggest office in the building enough reward?

In a sense, this is true. If anyone has control over their work, it's the head of the company. And the head of the company almost always cashes the biggest paycheck. However, as you know, this is a simplistic view of your position. After all, no one truly has control over a business. You may be able to call the big shots in your office, but you can't control supply chain issues, key employees leaving, recessions, restrictions set by the board, a new competitor rising up to take a big chunk of the market, or new technologies, government policies, or culture shifts that put pressure on your bottom line.

These are the problems that keep entrepreneurs up at night. And you have no control over any of them.

As my friend Kevin Christie says, there's a big difference between being the one signing the front of the check and being the one signing the back of it.

At the same time, after a certain point, that paycheck you're also signing on the back stops feeling like a reward, and the sense of achievement you used to feel can be subsumed in the problems of today—in the struggle to achieve the same level of scale you did previously or to keep up with expectations set by investors. Once your life adjusts to your level of success, you stop feeling that jolt of joy that used to keep you going. This is called "hedonic adaptation." And once that jolt is gone, all that's left is the grind of those tough days at work.

Consider the circumstances around the burnout of a client of mine, Joe. Joe runs a very successful business that is reliant on digital ads. He's managed his business very well, but none of that previous success felt like much of a reward when he faced a new crisis. Apple's new iPhone operating system allowed users to block the use of their data.

No user data, no targeted ads. No targeted ads, no business for my client.

It was a decision he had no part in, and one he could do nothing to reverse. It's no wonder he found it harder to find the energy to go into the office or to even say hello to those he saw in the hallway. This lack of control combined with the demanding nature of his work and the consequences for failing to meet this crisis left him feeling short-tempered, irritable, and dejected.

He also struggled to make those snap decisions that used to come so easily. Like a batter who has lost his confidence, starts overthinking his swing, and suddenly faces strikeout after strikeout, every decision Joe made, he second-guessed. Even when he tried not to think about it, he overthought it. He lost that gut instinct that had served him so well.

Joe was more successful than the vast majority of people, but due to the nature of his work, the stress he had accumulated up to that point made it difficult for him to face this new crisis. Instead of pivoting to a new strategy, the crisis left him feeling like a failure—and feeling like there was no way out.

It wasn't the crisis that overwhelmed him; it was years of demands, responsibilities, and struggling for control. By the time Facebook changed its policy, he was ripe for burnout. This just pushed him over that edge.

THE ENGINE FOR SUCCESS

Remember what it used to feel like going into the office? You lived to get to work every day. The challenges you faced were energizing, and you always seemed to find a solution almost effortlessly. In fact, a whole day could pass in the blink of an eye because you were so focused on the tasks at hand. On those days, it seemed as if you never put a foot wrong. And at the end of the day, when you came home exhausted and satisfied by your efforts, you felt, in a word, happy.

We often assume that it was the success that made us happy, but psychological studies have shown we have that backwards. In one metastudy that appeared in the Psychological Bulletin in 2005, Sonja Lyubomirsky, Laura King, and Ed Diener found that it is the happiness that makes us successful—across many areas of life. When we're happy, we are energetic. We're more willing to take on challenges and try new things. We feel creative and want to express ourselves. We're outgoing, and we have large reserves of patience and diligence to confront any troubles that might arise.

So while you might assume that your recent struggles at work are the reason you've felt less happy, it's likely the situation is the reverse. Your life was out of balance, which drained you of happiness and left you struggling in the office.

This distinction is important because, far too often, hard-nosed entrepreneurs are dismissive of the idea of happiness. They see themselves almost as ascetics, willing to forego things like happiness and contentment for the sake of success. They'll sacrifice almost anything to see their dreams achieved. This effort is often admirable, but dismissing happiness as inconsequential can affect the business they care so much for. If a lack of happiness in life leads to a lack of focus in the office, the business suffers with the entrepreneur.

Put another way, happiness is your engine for success. It provides the power you need to push your business forward. You'd never leave your engine in such disrepair that you'd risk a breakdown on the highway, yet that's precisely how you left your emotional and motivational engine. So if you want to get back to how it used to be in the office, it's time to start making some repairs.

RETURNING TO HAPPINESS

On that day in September, I sat in the dark, looking at a photo of my twin sister, Magdalena. She had died only a month before after a long struggle with brain cancer. Hers was an especially tragic story. The disease had struck her when she had just gotten her life on track. She had gone from work that she was good at—as a controller at a hedge fund run by our brother Rafael—to a job at the University of Richmond, where she was truly happy. She had four beautiful, young children, and thanks to the benefits at her new job, she would be able to send them all to college.

She was looking forward to a long life, raising the kids she loved and working at a job she loved.

When she got her diagnosis, she was several months short of receiving her benefits.

Still, through the worry, the disappointment, the sadness, the pain, and the fear, she managed to remain happy. There's no other word for it. Whenever we would talk, I could hear her smiling through the phone.

At first, there was optimism. "I'm going to beat this. It's going to be okay."

Even as the likeliness of a cure began to fade, she remained positive and upbeat. "It's not so bad. I get to be home with my kids."

In the last couple months, when she was really struggling, she still maintained her humor. When our brother Rafael visited her near the end, she burst out laughing, "I can't even get out of bed. Isn't this ridiculous?"

The picture I held that day reflected her untamable joyful attitude. In it, she was smiling ear to ear, wearing a wig because she was going through chemo. Looking at that photo, I realized that I owed it to her not to give up and submit to burnout. Her brave positivity in the face of far more serious circumstances than I could imagine gave me the courage to demand more from myself.

Something had to change. And her example would lead the way.

I made a commitment then and there to make that change. From that day, I started making slow, uncertain progress back from burnout. Through many false starts and unexpected cul-de-sacs, I brought together the inspiration of my sister, my decades of training and experience in psychiatry, the tools I'd acquired in Alcoholics Anonymous, the wisdom of classical thinkers, and the advice of the best life coaches. Eventually, reviewing my progress and failures, I was able to assemble a system that could bring me back to the happiness Magdalena had exemplified.

The result was the Happiness Rules. These rules allowed me—and will allow you—to take small, positive steps toward a healthier, more optimistic, and happier life. Through these rules, I regained my energy and the motivation to work. I stopped entertaining negative thoughts and started putting my health first on my list of priorities. I began to live intentionally and make mindful choices about what I needed and wanted from life. I recovered the ability to concentrate, and I saw new paths that could lead me out of my desperate situation.

As I progressed through these rules, I found out I wasn't trapped in a life without happiness and without opportunities. I found a new path, one that provided me with a new sense of success and a new drive to achieve. And through these rules, I found I could create a life that could flourish through any circumstances.

RESTARTING YOUR ENGINE

None of this is to say that the Happiness Rules solved every problem in my life. I still needed to find a way to make more money to cover my responsibilities. I still had numerous relationships to repair with family and friends. And while my love for psychiatry would return in time, it would never again be the center of my life as it had. I would soon discover there were other avenues I would need to explore if I wanted to feel like I was truly flourishing.

The same will prove true for you. The Happiness Rules won't fix your strained relationships or put extra money in your pocket, and they won't provide you with some brilliant, innovative solution to the problems in your office or your personal life.

In these pages, you will not find any treatment for physical or mental illnesses—this is not a way to treat depression or any other psychological condition. However, if you are feeling exhausted, bitter, detached from work, or seeing a lack of effectiveness in your work—or if you are feeling a lack of purpose, a sense of stagnation, or emotionally numb—the Happiness Rules can provide you with a consistent, healthier state of mind no matter what issues you are facing.

The tools in this book help alleviate burnout and provide a structure that will ensure it doesn't return again. If you follow the advice ahead, you can restart that engine that has driven you to success and maintain it in a way that is healthier for you, your business, and those you care about.

From feeling so hopeless at the prospect of continuing working that I contemplated suicide, these days, I'm so happy at work I've decided that I never want to stop working. I have the energy to not just get through the day but to expand my business. And I still have enough time and energy left over to work on those family relationships while strengthening my ties to the community.

I feel a greater sense of freedom in my actions because I am able to make positive choices in how I invest my time and effort. And I have organized my life to maintain that energy and freedom going forward. I still have my share struggles in work and in life, but my internal experience is so different that those struggles no longer have the ability to burn me.

Joe experienced a similar turn around. Once we started working through the Happiness Rules, he made a remarkable recovery to his former energy and optimism. He's now developed a solution to overcome the setback after Apple changed its policies, and he's thriving in his work once more.

This can be your future as well. No matter how hopeless your situation feels or how worn out you are, there is a way back to your previous sense of happiness and all the success it brought you.

But before you can follow the rules that lead you back, you have to first acknowledge where you are—and that you have a problem. You have to accept that you are facing burnout. That it isn't a weakness. That you're allowed to struggle. And that the consequences of ignoring this situation can be serious.

Only then can we commit to change and make our way back onto the path of happiness.

PART I

WHY WE NEED NEW RULES

THE COST OF BURNOUT

"'How did you go bankrupt?' Bill asked. 'Two ways,' Mike said. 'Gradually, then suddenly.'"

—ERNEST HEMINGWAY, *THE SUN ALSO RISES*

A psychiatric patient of mine, whom I'll call Jacob here to protect his privacy, was a landscape architect who designed beautiful outdoor areas for some of the richest and most famous people in the country. Jacob absolutely loved his job. It allowed him to express his creativity, earn a fantastic income, and hang out with the most glamorous people on the planet. His name was mentioned in elite circles as the person to speak to if someone wanted to create one of those properties you see in the magazines.

He had the kind of career and lifestyle that everyone wants. He had the house and the car and the family that people would give anything for. He had it all.

And it was making him sick.

His work was, by nature, high pressure. The deadlines were aggressive and non-negotiable, and the expectations of his high-paying clientele were overwhelming. He worked for people who demanded the best service, and he had to deliver every single day. At the same time, he had friction with his business partner. They no longer saw eye-to-eye on the direction the company should take. There were flare-ups at the office and tensions in their every interaction, and it all required energy that Jacob couldn't spare.

For years, he pushed on. He would wake up tired and still find a way to get into the office and get the work done. He stopped enjoying the parties and all the hobnobbing that had once seemed so appealing, but he kept socializing all the same.

Slowly, though, the burnout he was trying to overcome through willpower began having an effect on his work and his health. He couldn't concentrate or make those crucial decisions that had once made him the best in his industry. At the same time, he spiraled from exhausted and disillusioned to depressed and anxious.

"I didn't love what I was doing anymore," he later told me. "I was trapped. I couldn't walk away from the money. I couldn't walk away from the praise. But I couldn't do this anymore."

Jacob had let his burnout rage for so long, he had very limited options left. His mental health was so low, continuing to work would put him at risk of serious consequences. The relationship with his partner was broken beyond the point of repair. Ultimately, he had little choice but to leave the work he had loved. He and his wife decided to live on her salary.

They downsized, sold the house and the cars that everyone envied, and started over.

He had to walk away from it all—simply because he'd tried to tough his way through the early warning signs instead of listening to what his body and mind were telling him.

THIS ISN'T GOING TO GO AWAY

Jacob was an extreme case. Usually, mindful attention to burnout can allow individuals to return to their happier, healthier, and more productive selves without abandoning their work. That's only possible, however, if the person suffering from burnout recognizes that they can't will the burnout away—or ignore it, or work even harder now so they can take time off later.

This is a particularly difficult lesson for entrepreneurs. Entrepreneurs are, by nature, fixers. And we're often very stubborn fixers at that. We see it as our job to dig in and repair whatever isn't working in our businesses in order to reach optimum effectiveness. Under normal circumstances, this serves us well. Normally, the problems we face at work require a well-thought-out strategy and a lot of effort and determination to execute. Whether it's the work of pepping everyone up or finding that one great idea that will salvage a product launch, it's a matter of rising to the occasion and working through that solution. Our do-it-yourself-at-all-costs motivation to find and carry out solutions is the hammer we use on every nail that pops up in our business.

However, burnout isn't a nail. It isn't a standard problem that we can fix by concentrating on it and executing a strategy. Unlike other problems, we can't work through burnout while we ignore our underlying stress and exhaustion. That only makes it worse.

We have to look at burnout like an underlying injury to our body and mind. On episode 180 of the Tim Ferriss podcast, he interviewed a successful gymnastics coach named Coach Sommer. At one point in the interview, Tim started talking about a time he tweaked his wrist at home. After a few weeks, while traveling overseas, he was so desperate for a good workout, he went to the gym and re-aggravated his injury. Instead of stopping, he decided to push through the pain.

"I'm finishing this workout," he recounted.

Coach Sommer answered bluntly, "I thought you were smart."

That may seem a bit brusk, but the point was extremely important. Tim's way of dealing with an injured wrist was to ignore the pain and lean into finishing the workout no matter what. To an entrepreneur, that makes sense. We do that all the time; it's part of that special mix of qualities that lead to our success. When others would quit, we keep at it. This may give us a leg up in business, but it can come at a cost. In reality, when you have an injury, the last thing you want to do is push through the pain. The pain is your body telling you to stop and attend to the issue. Ignoring your body and forcing your way through the pain only leads to further injury.

The same is true of burnout. Burnout is your mind and body telling you to change what you're doing, not lean further into it. Ignoring the symptoms of burnout only makes the injury worse. Not only will we feel increasingly more exhausted, we will also lose the ability to think our way out of the situation. Our ever-increasing stress leads to poor judgment, a loss of introspection, and a weakened ability to make the best choices to relieve that stress. We develop tunnel vision in which all we do is work, and as far as we can conceive in that moment, there's no possibility to escape that tunnel. That sense of being trapped makes us bitter. We start to feel hopeless.

We enter a downward spiral, and the force pulling us down increases the further we fall. The further we fall, the more impossible it feels to find a means of escape.

This is the situation Jacob found himself in. By the time he came to me, he was so burned out by his circumstances, his once-world-class insight and creativity had been enfeebled to the point he could no longer be effective in his work. He could barely make it through a workday, yet his tunnel vision left him seeing no other options but to stubbornly march on.

The same was true of my own burnout experience. When I was spiraling into that dark moment in September 2008, there were many potential solutions available to me to relieve the big stressors on my life. I needed money, but I could have started another business. I could have focused on maximizing my investments or sold some assets. I could have negotiated with my ex-wives over alimony in order to cover some of the upcoming college expenses I would face. I could have brought in junior partners and taken a cut of their profits as we increased our client numbers. I could have hired an administrator to organize my schedule better to get the most value from my time.

But by then, I'd lost the ability to problem solve on that level. I was stuck in a pattern of overworking, but I couldn't see any way to change my circumstances. That tunnel vision closed out all of my remaining options. The only choice I felt I had was to keep going, even though I knew it wasn't sustainable. And that choice was only leading one direction: further down.

THE BURNOUT CONTINUUM

It may be that your experience of burnout doesn't compare to what you've read about Jacob or me. You aren't mulling over quitting your business or suicide. Perhaps you're just a little tired and frustrated with work. So what does all this dramatic talk of permanent injury and potential depression have to do with you?

Potentially, everything, if nothing changes. Burnout is on a continuum. In the early stages, you are still near your baseline, which is your emotional equilibrium. On most days and in most ways, you function normally, with a normal amount of energy, normal amount of creativity and focus, and normal levels of effectiveness. Some days are harder—in which you feel extremely tired, short-tempered, and not functioning at your highest level—but you can usually push through. You might still find that the majority of your days you'd count yourself relatively happy.

As your burnout shifts farther down the continuum, though, you grow more exhausted and more cynical, and that tunnel vision begins to creep in. You notice yourself snapping at employees, clients, friends, and family for the slightest provocation—and you seem to lack the energy to correct this. Slowly, you start more days feeling exhausted, and you end more days looking for ways to check out of your responsibilities, whether that entails leaving the office early or simply putting on Netflix from the moment you get home to the moment you go to bed. From having big dreams for yourself, your family, and your company, you may slowly become more pessimistic and myopic—life is all about work, and work is an unending challenge.

These shifts can be more subtle as well. You may see a shift toward pessimism in every area of your life as you fall under the sway of negative feelings of the moment instead of finding the reserves to maintain your energy and optimism. You may focus more on the things you don't have control over instead of those you can solve. You may externalize more problems and look for something or someone out there to blame for the change in your perspective. Suddenly, a bad meeting can't be brushed off so easily. It becomes a day-ruiner. A client call that doesn't result in a new sale gets mulled over for hours. A whole weekend can disappear under the cloud of a slight dip in profits.

Life comes with problems, and all of these are normal feelings. However, as you slide down the burnout continuum, these normal feelings begin to dominate your life. Where once you would have rebounded quickly and focused on how to fix these problems, now you simply dwell on the problem itself and how helpless you feel before it. Eventually, those good happy days become rare enough to feel like holidays. You cherish them precisely because they are so infrequent.

Unfortunately, that's only half the continuum. Once you are sliding down in this spiral, you're accelerating right toward those dramatic stories that seem so exaggerated right now. In fact, those events are far closer than they may seem at the moment.

THE POTENTIAL END

Injuries left untreated can become more severe over time. If you're a football fan, you undoubtedly have opinions about the NFL concussion policies. These policies have developed out of a growing body of evidence that multiple concussions sustained over a long period of time do significant damage to the brain. A player can "shake it off" once or twice and seem to be fine, but over time, those repeated injuries can become a condition called Chronic Traumatic Encephalopathy—which can cause memory loss, depression, dementia, and suicidality, among other things.

Burnout progresses in the same way. On its own, it is not serious enough to be considered a psychological disease. Instead, it's a prodrome, closer to a set of symptoms that can become disease over time. Left untreated, though, that prodrome can mature into disease, and if it does, the consequences are dire. Like Jacob, unattended burnout can turn into an anxiety disorder and or a major depressive disorder. Essentially, burnout can so overwhelm your system that your ability to function can be compromised to the point you require serious professional help. We're talking therapy and psychotropic medication. At its worst, burnout can eventually lead to such a profound sense of hopelessness that it can result in death by suicide.

This is only the psychological component. The end point

for unattended burnout can also affect your physical health. Chronic stress can cause all sorts of medical problems, including high blood pressure, heart conditions, and an increased risk of stroke.

Outside your immediate health, burnout can cause massive disruption to your personal life. At home, you may find you have nothing left to give to your relationships. You become emotionally distant. Over time, this emotional exhaustion can lead to divorce and estrangement from friends and your children.

Sometimes, as in Jacob's case, burnout can even lead to the inability to do the one thing you do best in the world: your work. Because you can't function at your highest level anymore, your business may struggle or even collapse. You may alienate your best clients and employees. From being the world's best boss, you can find that no one wants to work with you anymore.

In the end, then, allowing yourself to slide down the burnout continuum can result in losing everything you care about. Burnout can take your family and friends, your business, and your health. If you aren't facing these serious circumstances yet, that's wonderful. There's still time to prevent the worst from happening. But you have to start making the necessary changes now, so that you can get back to happiness and avoid paying a terrible price for delay.

THE BEGINNING CONNECTS TO THE END

I started going to Alcoholics Anonymous (AA for short) about twenty-five years ago. At that point, I'd been dancing around the fact that I had an alcohol problem for quite some time. Whenever my then-wife, Marlana, confronted me about my drinking, I always responded with the traditional excuses.

"I'm not drinking that much."

"I'm just stressed from work."

"This is how I unwind."

Finally, she put her foot down. It was her and the kids or the beer. I agreed to stop drinking cold turkey from that moment on. I made it two whole days without a drink. Then I snuck a beer. Strange as it may be to read this, I was actually immensely proud of myself. I had only had one beer. I stopped after one. See? No drinking problem here!

It was only when I repeated this in my head that I realized how pathetic it sounded. Worse than that, I started to see how my thinking was bordering on the delusional. I had promised my wife I wouldn't drink. She had said my drinking could end our marriage. And I was proud that I'd only betrayed her trust a little bit and snuck one beer. That's how powerful my justifications had become.

That's when I knew I had a problem.

It had been hard to come to terms with my alcoholism partly because I wasn't an alcoholic like you see in the movies. I wasn't getting kicked out of bars at closing time or selling my stuff to buy a bottle of booze. I was successful. I went to work every day and met all my obligations. Until that night, I had never hidden my drinking. I'd done it in front of everyone, and most of the people I knew never said a word about it.

This wasn't just a personal problem. AA has historically also found it difficult to help people see how the early stages of alcoholism that can be rationalized away lead directly to the late-stage alcoholism we can all recognize. The natural instinct most people have when they first go to an AA meeting is to listen for ways in which everyone else in the room is different from them. What they want to hear is that these people are alcoholics but *they* just enjoy having a drink sometimes. Everyone else has a problem; they're doing just fine. "I am not like *them.*"

The instinct is to exclude themselves from the label of alcoholic and the dark path that word suggests that they are on. This is part of the reason it's so hard to get people to go to a meeting in the first place. People don't want to face that kind of problem. It often takes some sort of external pressure to compel an alcoholic to attend their first meeting. Someone in their lives insists they go, as Marlana did with me, or some legal enforcement demands they attend. Once they're at the meeting, all they want to do is find some proof that they don't need it.

AA has countered this instinct to rationalize away alcoholism by tying those early-stage signs of a problem to the late-stage issues we all know. They have studied this extensively, and what they have done is create a system that emphasizes that most alcoholics have very similar early experiences. There was a test or a job interview or an important event to attend and instead of studying, preparing, or getting some rest, the alcoholic went to a party to drink—to just have one...that turned into six. There was a social event, and while everyone else had a couple drinks, the alcoholic got drunk.

When they face some consequences for their drinking, alcoholics come up with excuses. The test wasn't important. They didn't want that job anyway. The cop shouldn't have pulled them over in the first place; they were driving fine. And so what if they drank more than everyone else? They were just having a good time or blowing off steam.

As the problems—and the consequences—get worse, alcoholics develop coping mechanisms. They only drink when they eat or set a limit on the number of drinks they allow themselves on a night out. Or they only drink beer instead of spirits because they can usually stay relatively sober.

That's why AA centers this shared narrative at their meetings, so everyone who is there for the first time can see that wherever they are on the alcoholic continuum, they are certainly on it somewhere. In order to be effective, AA has to encourage people to identify with the other people in the room and recognize, "I'm just like them." As this reality sets in, a paradigm shift occurs, and denial clears away. Given the time and the conditions, an alcoholic who sneaks one beer when he promised not to drink at all can end up like those who will sell their coat in a blizzard for a bottle of cheap whiskey.

The same process has to occur with burnout. We have to come to terms with the fact that the mild symptoms of early burnout lead directly to the dark consequences of ignoring it. The amount of suffering that you can endure through burnout is comparable to alcoholism. And like alcoholism, it isn't something you have to suffer.

Famously, the first step in the Twelve-Step Program developed by AA is to admit there's a problem. That step has to come first because we can't address an issue until we face the seriousness of that issue. If you're in a car and the brakes go out at the stoplight, you don't keep driving that car just because you survived. You get that car towed and get new brakes. We need to trigger that same response with burnout. When we start seeing warning signs for burnout, we can't dismiss them. We can't ignore them. We can't fight them. We have to address the problem as soon as possible.

In alcoholism, the lines are clear. If you continue to drink in the face of negative consequences, you have a problem. There's a clear prognosis. The disease is progressive, so if you don't deal with it, things will get worse. But burnout isn't so different. If you continue to push yourself and work harder in the face of increasing exhaustion, fraying relationships, and a growing sense of pessimism and dissatisfaction, there's a problem.

And the sooner you deal with it, the more likely you will be able to avoid the scenario Jacob faced. The first time your spouse says you are no longer emotionally available enough for the family or the first day you really can't get up and go into work, that's the time to address your burnout. The first time you blow up at an employee for a minimal mistake or feel a deep sense of hopelessness, that's when you should look to make a change.

I know that isn't an easy step to take. Like alcoholism, it's hard to face a problem when society tells you that it's okay. Everyone drinks! You're just having a good time! You only live one life! And society is telling you as an entrepreneur that working yourself to the bone is admirable, even exemplary.

But if you want to regain your happiness and restart the engine that drove you to success, you're going to have to recognize that society is wrong.

THE GIST

For those too busy to read through the entire book and for those coming back to these chapters for a quick review, these "gists" will give you the main points to take away from each chapter.

Here, we looked at the nature of burnout. There is a continuum of burnout. Ignoring early, mild signs—such as exhaustion, feeling detached or negative about work, or losing effectiveness at work—will lead to these issues getting worse.

There's an inclination to find ways to deny that this is happening. As they point out in AA, many will seek evidence that they are "not like them" instead of the evidence that this is happening. That is, they look for differences instead of the significant similarities.

We have to face the truth about burnout. Over time, burnout spreads to affect not just work but the rest of your life, from family and friends to health.

WHY BURNOUT IS SO PREVALENT

Part of my training during psychiatric residency involved interviewing and evaluating new patients when they were starting treatment at one of our clinics. These clinics dealt with serious psychiatric conditions, and it was my job to start the process by evaluating the new patient and coming up with a diagnosis and treatment plan when they were admitted to the anxiety clinic, mood disorder clinic, or psychosis clinic.

I would begin these interviews with a standard opening question: "What brings you in today?" Frequently, the first words out of their mouth were, "I feel terrible. I want to feel better. I want to be happy again."

When I first encountered this response, I reported it to my supervisor.

"The patient's chief complaint is that she isn't happy."

My supervisor shook his head. "Treating for happiness is not what we do here. We can treat a patient's depression symptoms; we can treat their anxiety symptoms or their psychosis; but we can't treat for happiness. We can't help someone be happy."

That event played through my mind often when I was burned out. If I had been suffering from depression again, I'd know right where to go. The same would be true if I were struggling with alcoholism again. But where was I supposed to go if I wasn't happy and couldn't perform at the level I used to? It didn't seem like there was anywhere to turn. Who was going to treat me for a lack of happiness?

CURRENT RESOURCES DON'T FOCUS ON HAPPINESS

Society offers plenty of tools for us when we're feeling overwhelmed. There's therapy, vacations, and meditation—and all of those are useful. You won't read one word against any of those options in this book. However, none of them are particularly designed to address the circumstances and mindsets that have led you to this place, so none of them can really bring you back to the happiness that you've misplaced.

Therapy, as I'll discuss in more depth in a moment, is still largely focused exclusively on psychological trauma and disorders. If you are facing any of those issues, by all means, you should enter therapy. However, while positive psychology—which sets its sights directly on well-being—has helped broaden this focus, therapy, as it is currently conceived, doesn't adequately address burnout.

So what about vacations? Those are wonderful, and if you can take one, by all means, do so. However, a vacation is somewhat like taking pain medication for a back injury. It can temporarily reduce or even remove the pain, but it doesn't treat the condition.

Likewise, mindfulness courses and meditation are excellent tools to deal with stress—and I recommend them—but neither provides a holistic system to address all the pressures in your life. Meditating while burned out won't solve the problem.

These are all powerful and valuable tools that can help you on your way back from burnout, but none of them truly address your needs because, unfortunately, our current conception of medicine and health is limited, and burnout simply doesn't fit into that system.

MEDICINE AND SOCIETY AREN'T EQUIPPED FOR BURNOUT

At the hospital where I did my residency, our primary concerns were medical. We were looking for medical conditions in patients that we could treat. By definition, for a medical condition to exist, there has to be a significant departure from health. A broken bone is a departure from a healthy bone, and we can fix that. Likewise, depression or anxiety is a departure from your otherwise healthy psychological baseline, and through a combination of psychotherapy and medication, we can raise you back to that baseline.

This is an extremely useful system, but it has its limitations. In particular, it leaves a massive blind spot when confronting issues that don't quite match the definition of medical condition, such as a reduction in level of energy or sense of hopefulness about the future. If these symptoms fall far enough that they can be defined as causing a decrease in functioning or a significant amount of psychological distress—and they meet a defined number of "criteria" for each condition—they would be diagnosed as a psychiatric disorder. But when they simply start drifting down from previous high levels of functioning, there's little medicine has to say about it other than "come back if it gets worse."

Currently in medicine, we are great at treating sickness, but we are not nearly as good at improving wellness or providing preventive sustainable care. There are far fewer tools to address increasing levels of stress when going to work if those levels don't reach anything we could categorize as clinical anxiety. Likewise, an ever-shortening fuse when dealing with confrontation won't receive much treatment until you hit a breaking point. In other words, when the question isn't returning to your baseline but raising a slowly sinking baseline, medicine has few answers.

And that's just where burnout fits. As we've already seen, burnout *can* lead to medical conditions, but it is not one in and of itself. Instead, the World Health Organization defines burnout as an occupational syndrome. A syndrome is less defined than a disease, which has established causes and symptoms, and causes consistent changes in the body. Because syndromes are less well defined with symptoms that are not as consistent, and causes that are often less clear, medicine struggles to target them—and thus traditionally offers fewer treatment options.

Medicine doesn't have to work this way, of course. It could expand its scope beyond the return to baseline. However, there have traditionally been few incentives to make this happen. Since the 1940s, medicine has been funded through health insurance reimbursement. However, health insurance pays for treatment when you are sick. Since burnout doesn't meet criteria for an actual disease and can't be targeted and treated by traditional medical practices, insurance usually won't pay. Where treatment does occur, it is under the diagnosis of diseases, such as depression or anxiety. If your insurance won't pay for a treatment designed to target burnout, the developers of medical advancements can't make a profit, and so such potential advancements don't get researched, tested, or brought to market. The system therefore has significant lag in developing ways to improve your baseline.

You can get an insurance payout when medicine heals you when you're sick, but it almost never happens when it comes to making you a better, happier person. If you have depression or anxiety, chances are, your insurance will cover at least some treatment, but if you want to improve your patience as a parent, become a more attentive spouse, increase your decisiveness as a leader, or simply feel like a more purposeful person, that's not going to be covered under most policies.

Because of the limitations in our methods and the insurance system, modern medicine is incentivized to make a quick diagnosis instead of looking for a root cause. The system prefers a diagnosis like depression or anxiety and a pill for treatment rather than a syndrome that is harder to quantify. There are many gifted clinicians and psychotherapists out there trying to push beyond these shortcomings in the system, but far too often, entrepreneurs with burnout simply fall through the cracks.

GOOD LEADERS GET BURNOUT

Most entrepreneurs strive to be good leaders. They want to motivate their teams, innovate their industry, inspire their customers, and push their companies to the limit. Unfortunately, the very qualities that allow an entrepreneur to do all this are the ones that make them most at risk of burnout.

The reason for this is that good leadership tends to expose you to all four of the pressures that lead to burnout:

- High demand
- High responsibility
- Low control
- Low reward

A good leader faces these pressures every day—in abundance.

Consider the high demand you are under. You have to work long hours every single day, and you never have easy days. The tasks that reach your desk are always the hardest problems that no one else below you could fix. Anything easily solved gets solved before you ever hear about it. This also means your solutions are often messy and complex and leave at least one party unhappy. When you're dealing with interpersonal disputes between managers, competition between departments, the truly tough and unappeasable customers, and products that are failing far beyond projections, it's hard to ever get a clear, definitive "win."

When you find the best possible solution available and move it off your desk, there's always another issue waiting for your attention. Your inbox is always full, you're always behind, and the next difficulty is always more serious than the last.

It would be nice to delegate some of this demand, but again, this is the nature of your work. You live in a world of high responsibility. The buck has to stop with you. Even when a problem is handed to one of your teams, you have to take ultimate responsibility for their decisions and actions. If anything goes wrong, you'll be the face of the mistake.

Ultimately, you are responsible for everything that happens in the entire company, and you have a responsibility to everyone under you to make the best possible choices in every situation. This is what you signed up for, but that doesn't make it any easier to face that pressure day-in and day-out.

Combine this with the low control you have over events: teams make mistakes; the economy takes swings up or down; just-in-time deliveries arrive just too late; competitors secure better funding; the government changes oversight priorities; technology evolves; clients develop new strategies that cut your business out; and new competitors rise up out of nowhere.

For all the freedom your position is meant to offer, so much is out of your hands—and that is a very difficult position to be in when you have so much demand on your attention and so much responsibility.

Of course, all of this can be relieved if you receive the right rewards for your efforts—but again, there are no clear "wins" for a good leader. Sure, you are likely well-compensated, but over time, money stops being the reward it once was. This is "hedonic adaptation" once again, diminishing your pleasure after you attain something. At some point, compensation stops making you happy like it used to.

Many have experienced this on vacation. If you are ever lucky enough to have the opportunity to take a long vacation, at some point on that perfect trip you'll start to notice that you're enjoying the trip a little less each day. Over time, you realize that you'd rather be home and back doing the daily tasks you left behind. You fill your cup with relaxation and paradise, and suddenly, it offers less happiness than it did at first.

Perhaps you're so overworked, you don't know that feeling. But it's the same one that comes with getting settled into a new car or a new house. At first, it's the greatest thing you've ever purchased and a center point for your happiness. Look at this incredible thing I purchased! Before long, though, it becomes normal, and it stops giving you the joy it once did. Then, you either buy a better car or a bigger home or else simply lose that sense of happiness entirely.

When you remove the enjoyment you used to get from your income, possessions, and stock options, you start feeling less rewarded for all that effort and sacrifice you are making. This is especially true of good leaders who make a habit of sharing or even giving away credit on the occasions they do earn a solid win. When something goes wrong, a good leader takes the blame, and when it goes right, they say someone else should be congratulated.

That's a very inspiring type of leadership, but it leaves you with a serious problem. How do you fuel the engine that allows you to handle all this high-demand, high-responsibility, low-control labor you do? At some point, the fuel simply runs out. And from firing on all cylinders, you begin to burn out.

A SOCIALLY ACCEPTED ADDICTION

Working this hard and under these circumstances clearly isn't good for us, but we keep it up not only because we feel a responsibility to do so, nor simply because it is our passion. In part, we push ourselves so hard that we tumble into burnout because that level of commitment to our work is prized by our society.

Hard work has become the defining characteristic deserving of praise in our society. Consider all the movies that have been made about the person who becomes a success simply through grit and extra effort: *Rudy*, *Rocky*, *The Pursuit of Happyness*. Intelligence, creativity, and skill can sometimes be lauded, but they are just as likely to be seen as wasted if not paired with hard work. Think of all the athletes who are either praised or criticized on their work ethic depending on how well they are playing. Our society has developed a conception that the difference between success and failure is not circumstance or even talent but simply how hard a person is willing to work for what they want.

And nowhere is this clearer than in the stories we tell ourselves about business. It's absolutely true that it takes a lot of work to get a business up and running, but this is rarely seen as a practical requirement. Instead, it's more of an ethos. The conception we've developed of a successful businessperson is one that never sleeps, never rests, and never tires. They live and breathe for business. This is not normal amounts of hard work and toughness we expect out of ourselves; it is often superhuman.

In the effort to live up to this ideal, we forget that the goal after all the hard work of getting the business off the ground is "freedom" and instead handcuff ourselves to jobs.

We're introduced to these values at a young age. Our school systems are not designed to encourage children to follow their interests or develop according to their natural aptitudes but to keep up with a grueling learning and testing regime. Those who sacrifice more and study hardest are praised. Those who follow more natural child-like instincts and engage in play are told they should be more serious about their studies.

Our society is obsessed with the idea of getting into the most competitive, difficult colleges—mostly just for the sake of it. One of my children went to Williams College, and he told me that many of his fellow students would brag about how little they slept before a test or before a big paper was due. It was a badge of honor to be sleep deprived throughout the school week. Then, they'd go out and binge drink right after their final class for the week.

And that's the other side of this system: When you work that hard, you need a release, and often those releases are at least as unhealthy as the hard work itself.

Amazingly, none of these efforts or habits leads to happiness, at least according to Shawn Achor. Achor studied burnout among students at Harvard University. He worked with some of the most brilliant and privileged students in the country. They were young, healthy, and studying at one of the great institutions of learning in the world. They were destined for great careers and financial success. They had everything going for them. And like Jacob in the last chapter, they were miserable.

They were so focused on driving themselves to the absolute top of the class list, they were really driving themselves into misery.

Perhaps that misery stems from the fact this expectation is so unnatural. Despite how pervasive the connection between hard work and success is in our society, it is not innate to human society. In previous eras, humans were largely driven by a desire to fulfill their role within their community. The intensity of an individual's work was less important than the fact they were contributing. Happiness was defined not by wealth or objects attained through hard work but through strong relationships and a place of importance within the society.

Hard work was, of course, expected at times in such systems. A farmer would still have to spend many hours plowing fields and gathering crops. A fisherman would still work hard to provide fish for the community. But the fisherman was not lauded for spending an extra three hours on the boat so he could add a room to his hut.

Of course, there were drawbacks to this ancient system—these societies required a certain level of conformity and limited independence; they didn't work for everyone—and I'm not trying to insist that we roll back the clock and artificially recreate this societal expectation. But it's important to recognize just how unnatural our current conception of work is. And not only unnatural, but unhealthy.

Workaholism is perhaps our society's only sanctioned addiction—made all the worse by the fact that society doesn't recognize it as a problem. Our culture struggles with burnout precisely because we elevate and reward hard work above all else. And like with any addiction, we do this in spite of evidence it is hurting us, until it advances to a degree where we lose control and cannot stop.

However, just because this is a societally endorsed trait, does not mean we have to endorse it ourselves. We can recognize our work addiction and call it what it is. And we can seek more constructive ways to achieve happiness. Those students at Harvard are not required to judge success by being top of class. They could just as easily grade themselves on the friends they make at the college—often more important to career and financial success anyway—or the quality of their educational experience, or the opportunities their education is offering to give back.

The same is true for entrepreneurs. Entrepreneurs are attracted to the idea of getting out of the system and setting their own standards, but far too often, they still judge themselves by the system's standards. They judge their success—and their happiness—by how fast they are scaling their business or how close their company is to five stars on Google Reviews. They judge their personal worth based on how much sweat they are pouring into those metrics.

They go into business to achieve freedom and instead create the hardest job they'll ever have. Then they lose sight of the metrics that might actually make it worthwhile. Instead of setting their own hours, they wake up at 4:00 a.m. to answer the first 400 emails of the day. Instead of expressing themselves through their business, they become slaves to paperwork. Where they want emancipation from strict schedules, they instead surrender weekends and holidays to push the company—and themselves—that little bit harder.

In other words, entrepreneurs are at once the people most likely to see through the superficial metrics within the system and to swallow them wholeheartedly.

But you don't have to think like this. You can redefine what success and happiness means for you and your business. More than anyone else, you can change the rules of the game if you choose.

ADOPTING LONG-TERM THINKING

To break free from the societal obsession with hard work above all else, we have to change how we think about our actions. Hard work over self-care often makes sense in a world of short-term thinking, and nowhere is this as clear as in business. Entrepreneurs are trained to prioritize short-term gains over long-term strategies. As Clayton Christensen pointed out in his book, *The Innovator's Dilemma*, the reason floppy disk companies didn't invest in thumb drives isn't because they were fools, it was because their priorities were always on the next quarter's profits. How could they justify years of research and development on an unproven technology when a slightly better floppy disc would give them profits now? Their job was to push for that slightly better disc as quickly as they could for as cheaply as they could, not to nurture the growth of a new technology that might be years away.

This is precisely how entrepreneurs conceive of their personal resources. Often, entrepreneurs focus on the short-term needs of the moment. There are projects they feel they have to get over the line immediately. There are meetings and conferences that have to be attended. On any given day, there's no time to focus on family time or personal health. You can't budget in the eight hours you need for sleep or even the extra hour you need for a decent lunch or a conversation with your family and friends.

How can you justify that when that short-term goal has to be reached as quickly as possible?

Unfortunately, while this kind of short-term thinking is understandable in the high-stress, high-stakes world of entrepreneurship, it's also a great way to burn yourself out. Eventually, those short-term decisions result in long-term costs. In the same way disc companies eventually failed because of short-term investment strategies, your health can fail because of those short-term priorities.

Eventually, on a longer timescale, those short-term choices can result in poor mental and physical health, divorce, bad relationships with our kids, and a general sense of isolation from our work, our community, and our lives. We end up stressed out, worn out, and burned out. In the same way one cheeseburger is a delicious meal but a cheeseburger a day for ten years can lead to a heart attack, so too the decisions you make—fueled by your society-approved workaholic tendencies—may lead to short-term positive results, but the cost is always coming.

To avoid those costs, we have to adjust our thinking and start prioritizing our long-term happiness over some of those short-term demands.

SMALL INVESTMENTS PAY OFF OVER TIME

Obviously, changing our conception of work and reprioritizing those long-term demands that can so easily be pushed off is not easy. As entrepreneurs, we face a constant demand for our time and energy and consistent approval when we choose work over other obligations. When we exhaust our resources and have nothing left for ourselves, we're praised by society. As soon as we have a free moment, a short-term problem arises to fill that time. As our energy and enthusiasm flags, society offers little relief—at least not until our health truly begins to suffer.

It's no wonder, then, that you're feeling burned out. How could it be otherwise?

And how can you change it?

If you don't want to walk away from your business, you are always going to have these short-term demands. And try explaining to investors or customers that you are de-prioritizing hard work in your life. It isn't going to go over well. Such sudden, radical change is impossible in the entrepreneurial world. The good news is that you don't have to throw away your business or refuse to take control in a crisis in the office. Through the Happiness Rules, you can take small steps to create slow, steady change for the better.

These small changes will pay off over time, increasing your energy and commitment to your work, so that you are a better entrepreneur who is capable of making better decisions and working as hard as the business requires. You don't have to make a choice between success and happiness. You can have both—if you're willing to start working on it now.

THE GIST

In an effort to be happy and fulfilled, we chase success. Society tells us from a young age that hard work is the key to this success.

This is wrong, and our focus upon work above all else is unhealthy. There is a point at which working hard can cross a line into addiction—defined as continuing to engage in an activity in spite of evidence that it is hurting you. When we eventually face burnout, society has few ways to bring us back to health and satisfaction.

Modern medicine is good at treating a disease, but burnout is an occupational syndrome and we don't have a treatment model for it.

There are four pressures that lead to burnout:

- Highly demanding work
- High level of responsibility
- Low control
- Low reward

Entrepreneurs are exposed to all four.

THE HAPPINESS RULES PREAMBLE

"Faith is taking the first step even when you don't see the whole staircase."

—MARTIN LUTHER KING

One patient from my residency days has stuck with me for my entire career. Her name was Sharon. She was a worn-out woman working two jobs and taking care of four children on her own. There was abuse in her background and a history of addiction in her family. She was grinding her life away trying to make ends meet, and as you might expect, she was simply exhausted.

My heart obviously went out to her. Confronting her circumstances as a second-year resident, I felt unable to offer her what she needed. How could I help a woman who clearly needed more assistance than a psychiatrist could offer? All I could do was give her a little judgment-free compassion and take an interest in her, her life, and her struggles.

Yet, surprisingly, that turned out to mean quite a lot to her.

At the end of her first session with me, she said, "Thank you. I feel so much better."

Though Sharon was a very unique woman, her response was not unique in the slightest. By that point in my training, my fellow residents and I had stumbled upon a curious fact about our work. Simply listening to someone during their initial evaluation, we'd often encounter that same response.

People started feeling better.

At first, I found this rather confusing. After all, I hadn't really *done* anything. I had administered no medicine and provided no treatment. My supervisor had an explanation for this: hope.

"Never underestimate the healing power of hope," he told me. And he was right.

Simply by listening without judgment and giving Sharon a name for what she was going through—something that she now knew others were going through, too—I had offered her the spark of hope she needed to regain a little of her strength. And when combined with a strategy back to health, that little bit of hope can make all the difference.

THREE THINGS TO KNOW RIGHT NOW

The first two chapters of this book painted a very negative picture of where your health is right now. We've seen the long-term damage burnout can do and how society, our business obligations, and our own personalities drive us towards that dark destination. However, that future isn't inevitable. Your situation is not hopeless. No matter where you are on the burnout spectrum, the Happiness Rules can help pull you out of it.

With that in mind, there are three facts I want you to recognize about yourself and your situation right now before we go any further:

- You are not alone
- Change is possible
- There is hope

Each of these concepts is an integral mindset adjustment on the road to happiness and becoming a better, healthier entrepreneur.

Now that you know that you are struggling with burnout and just how serious burnout is, it's time to start the journey to overcoming it. To make any headway in your struggle with burnout, you have to start by recognizing you aren't alone. Burnout is a very common problem, particularly (although by no means exclusively) in entrepreneurs. However, even if you accept that point, that knowledge is still likely quite conceptual. In the midst of burnout, you can feel alone in these feelings. This is also the case with alcoholism. Twenty-two years ago, when I hit rock bottom with my drinking, perhaps the most overwhelming feeling I experienced was loneliness.

And it's hard to feel any hope or like anything can change when you feel alone.

Among its other characteristics, alcoholism brings with it a deep sense of shame, and the effort to hide that struggle can feel isolating. I became so focused on keeping my illness a secret, I drove thirty miles away for my first AA meeting, to a men's only group in Albany, where I knew no one would recognize me. I was so desperate for understanding, however, that when I raised my hand to introduce myself, I ended up saying far more about myself than I ever meant to. I told the group that I was a psychiatrist and where my practice was. I opened up and talked about things I hadn't talked about with anyone before—things that brought me shame and that laid heavily on my conscience. This obviously defeated the purpose of driving so far away to remain anonymous. If anyone had wanted to look me up, they would have had all the information they needed—and plenty of secrets to hold against me.

But I've never regretted being so open on that Saturday morning because of the man I met there. After the meeting ended, a guy wearing a dress shirt and slacks came up and shook my hand.

"My name is Bryan," he said. "And I'm a psychiatrist, too. One of the things you will realize coming to these meetings is that we've all been through what you're going through. You don't have to be alone anymore."

Simple words, but they made me want to cry. To feel like someone else had lived through these difficulties and come out the other side elevated me off that rock-bottom floor I'd been stuck on. It was the lifeline I needed to keep going.

It's the same with burnout. While suffering from it, you may feel you're the only successful entrepreneur going through this, but I promise you, if I gathered all the entrepreneurs in your area, you'd find plenty going through the same thing right now—and plenty of others who have made it through and rediscovered happiness in their work and personal lives.

Implicit in the recognition you are not alone is the belief that you can change. Things can get better. After all, people don't go to AA for the camaraderie—that's secondary—they go to change so that their tomorrow is better than today. The trickiest thing about change is that we have to believe it is possible before it becomes possible.

Years ago, in my own period of burnout, I came across the story of Becky Douglas. After the death of her daughter, Amber, by suicide, Becky felt like her own life was over. Yet, she discovered over time that new purpose was possible, even in that horrific circumstance. It started when she and her husband went to clean up her room. While sorting Amber's possessions into boxes, they discovered that she had been sending some money to an orphanage in India. To further this generosity, Becky's family asked mourners to send donations to the orphanage instead of flowers. Those donations led to a role on the orphanage board, which further led to Becky visiting India and encountering leprosy colonies for the first time, where leprosy patients and their families were exiled and left to fend for themselves, largely by begging.

Becky responded to this experience by founding a charity. She brought medical supplies into the leprosy colonies and established a system of microloans for the women in those villages so they could go out and buy the tools they needed to start making money. She brought in teachers from America to improve teaching methods in the community. She helped establish a soccer team and flew out Broadway stars to start a dance troupe.

All of this was only possible because, as Becky believed, as she put it, "change is possible." When she started, she was simply a grief-stricken mother who didn't know how to send an email. Because she was open to change, her life today is almost unrecognizable from that low moment.

Of course, change like that is only possible if we not only believe it but pursue it. That is where the final piece fits into this. We have to be willing to hope for that change. That was the power that allowed Sharon to keep going despite her difficult circumstances. It was the power that kept me going to AA. And it was the power that fueled Becky's transformation.

It seems so simple, but the secret ingredient to seizing upon change and overcoming burnout really is as basic as the recognition that there is hope—even for you.

WHERE WE'RE HEADED

But what are we hoping for? Where are these Happiness Rules supposed to take us?

The obvious answer is "to happiness," but I know that isn't necessarily compelling for many entrepreneurs. They'd rather sacrifice happiness in order to see their business grow and their dreams achieved. However, these two concepts go hand-in-hand. Raising your baseline happiness doesn't just leave you more content with your personal life, it can also improve your performance in the workplace. Overcoming burnout and embracing a happier lifestyle can have a number of positive effects on an entrepreneur. It can lead to:

- Higher energy levels
- Fewer missed days and half-days of works
- Increased decisiveness and incisiveness
- Greater engagement with work priorities
- Improved focus and attention
- Clearer goals that provide reward for you and others in your organization
- Greater resilience to setbacks
- Deeper intimacy with customers, employees, and personal relationships

And this is only the beginning. There are also health benefits to the Happiness Rules. You can permanently reduce stress, which leads to not only lower risks for cardiovascular disease and many chronic physical diseases as you age but better control over your temper and more endurance for those long, difficult days in the office. Instead of wasting time and energy on physical or mental health concerns that arise due to a lack of attention to yourself, that time and energy can be reinvested in work and your personal life.

In other words, the Happiness Rules can provide you with a clear path to success in your work and throughout your life. And they can help you maintain that new level of happiness no matter what happens. They can provide not only relief from burnout but a future in which burnout is no longer a possibility.

The key here is recognizing that happiness is the engine that fuels your success. Happiness doesn't result from success; it creates that success. That's the power of becoming happy again.

To get to that future, we'll need to take several crucial steps towards happiness. That starts with a set of Health Rules that address your physical and mental health. Once we've set you on a course to improve those areas, we will take on the Growth Rules that help us grow into happiness through establishing habits of life-long learning and broadening our connections and finding our place within a community. Finally, we will use the Purpose Rules to create happiness that strengthens resilience when facing future struggles by committing, to blazing our own trail and enjoying the ride, no matter what life throws at us.

With these rules in place, you can create that sustained sense of burnout-resistant happiness for the rest of your life.

And that is something worth hoping for.

THE GIST

As we learned in Chapters 1 and 2, burnout is not something to ignore. But that is no reason to give up. Instead, remember these three things:

- You are not alone
- Change is possible
- There is hope

To overcome your burnout, we'll find the way back to happiness through three sets of rules:

- Health Rules
- Growth Rules
- Purpose Rules

PART II

THE HEALTH RULES

GETTING YOUR BODY INTO SHAPE

"I have always believed that exercise is the key not only to physical health but to peace of mind."

—NELSON MANDELA, *LONG WALK TO FREEDOM*

My brother Rafael is the definition of a high achiever. I may have done alright for myself in the entrepreneurial world, but Rafael has blown away my achievements in business. He founded his own hedge fund, and over the course of his very successful career, he's made a lot of his investors rich. All that success, though, made it hard to ever catch his breath. He was always in demand and immensely busy. For years, every time I called him, he'd always be traveling. There was always some client or new potential investor he needed to meet with.

When your schedule is that packed, it's hard to ever find the time to take care of yourself. Something always has to give, and for Rafael, that was his health. He couldn't justify the extra hour in his day to get to the gym. Beyond that, he didn't focus on what he was putting into his body. He overate and was at an unhealthy weight. Over time, always putting business before his physical health led to some consequences. The days seemed to exhaust him in a way they never had before. He grew crankier. And even though he loved what he did, he became less satisfied in his work.

Instead of letting himself descend into burnout, though, my proactive brother decided to make a change. He flipped his priorities and started forcing time to work out into his schedule. This one choice led to a profound change in not just his physical but his emotional well-being. His energy levels rebounded to their highest-ever level, and he found he had much more patience with others.

He was so pleased with his early improvement, he began scheduling his workouts at times when he could have otherwise been making money. Where he would once have rushed out the door at his hotel in whatever city he was visiting, in an effort to squeeze in one more potential client, he now made the decision to build working out into his daily schedule. He'd take an extra hour for himself, even if it cost him that extra client.

However, that choice has led to improved focus and endurance, which has almost certainly actually raised his bottom line more than those extra meetings would have. Rafael made a trade off, and as usual, he clearly got the better end of that deal.

HEALTH IS THE FOUNDATION OF HAPPINESS

Ask any architect, and they'll tell you that you can't build much of anything if you don't have a solid foundation underneath. Trying to build a mansion on shifting ground is a recipe for a very expensive construction disaster. Likewise, you can't build a structure that supports sustained happiness without the proper foundation in place first—and that foundation is your physical and mental health.

Put bluntly, it is incredibly difficult to be happy and a successful entrepreneur if your fundamental physical and mental health is out of order.

In fact, solidifying the foundations of your physical and mental health can arrest your slide into burnout, as Rafael discovered. Even if you are more deeply entrenched in burnout than Rafael was, by strengthening these foundations, you can get some quick wins on the way back to your baseline.

That was certainly my experience. The first thing I did after the photo of my sister, Magdalena, inspired me to try to overcome my burnout was to work on improving my physical and mental health. I realized that there was nothing I could immediately do to impact the pressures at the heart of my burnout. I couldn't cut down on my long hours at work or the financial stresses of providing for my family anytime soon, but I could change what I ate and how much sleep I got.

There was a lot in my life that felt out of my control, but adjusting my unhealthy routines and habits was something I could choose to do. And that, in and of itself, felt pretty good.

WHY WE PUT OFF THE BASICS

We all know that we should pay more attention to our health. At this point, there may not be a person in America who is unaware of how important it is to eat well, exercise, and get an adequate amount of sleep.

So why don't we do it? As the entrepreneur and author Jim Rohn once said, "Things that are easy to do are also easy not to do." In other words, we are very good at finding excuses to avoid doing what we know we should do. After all, we live extremely busy lives, and we have a number of obligations. Making choices with the short-term urgency discussed in Chapter 2 can leave us always putting aside the seemingly easy things we could do to improve our health.

We'd like to go for a long walk, but we have some files to review. We'd love to cook a nice, healthy dinner, but we're just too tired after that string of meetings during the work-day. Sleep sounds great, but who can blame us for staying up watching sitcoms and numbing out after such a long day?

I don't mean to be judgmental here. It is actually incredibly hard to prioritize our long-term needs. And that is at least in part because this is the first time in history when we have had to consciously make health a priority.

Consider the struggle many of us experience when we try to start regularly working out. On a superficial level, our constant excuses and delays can look like laziness, but it's really a lack of adaptation to our new circumstances as a species. For almost the entirety of human existence, our basic needs required us to work our bodies. To simply feed ourselves and provide shelter, we had to hunt or farm or wander around looking for berry bushes. To get anywhere, most of us had to walk, often many miles in a day. If I needed water to clean myself or to cook, I had to walk to the well, pull the water out, and carry it home. If I wanted bread, I had to walk to the mill, drag the grain back, and then spend hours cooking. The only motivation needed for physical activity was survival.

It's only been in the last one hundred years that those circumstances have changed for most of us. Now that you don't have to work your body to survive, you have to develop a reason to move it, and many of us simply don't want or know how to do that. All that convenience we have in the present day is great, but it does make it hard to find the motivation to get up and move around. Think of all you can do while sitting down! You can order food and have it delivered to your door, watch a million movies, listen to any song ever recorded, and play any number of thousands of entertaining video games. You can even do your shopping from your screen and have any product brought to you. In fact, it's often not only convenient but cheaper to live like this. Amazon prices often beat those of the store you'd have to get up and go to. So why move at all, particularly after a long, hard day?

And our days *are* hard. We work long hours and are expected to be far more productive than our ancestors. Though we don't work physically, our minds are exhausted by the amount of information they have to process. So when we get to the end of our day, our brains are tired, our bodies are unexercised, and we lack that motivation to move to survive.

Our society doesn't make this any easier on us, either. Most of us don't live in places with enough public transportation or population density to walk everywhere. When we do leave the house, we have to sit down and drive. It takes a small number of steps to get from the car to either the couch or the desk chair in the office. From there, you really only need to get up to feed yourself or use the toilet.

None of this is meant to dissuade you from attending to your health—far from it. We all know people who have found a way to maintain health under these circumstances. And the solution to achieving that level of health doesn't involve wacky diets or extreme fitness regimens. It takes something far easier: making health improvements one step at a time.

LITTLE STEPS

We're often presented with a false choice when we want to improve our physical health: either go out and join P90X and go all in on a Keto diet starting tomorrow or else accept that you're stuck with an unhealthy lifestyle. Undeniably, some small percentage of people really do take those more extreme life changes, but healthier living certainly doesn't require such drastic action. In fact, smaller, incremental changes are often far more likely to stick.

The problem with big, bold steps is that most people quickly become discouraged. True, you might be motivated enough to sign up for rigorous programs and spend a week or two working out every day and following all the dietary guidelines. But shortly after that positive start, most people start to feel overwhelmed and discouraged. They're tired all the time. Their muscles hurt. They're hungry. And are they really seeing results that justify all this effort?

At that point, the vast majority of people quit. After all, we haven't evolved to work our bodies this hard when survival isn't on the line. So while that intense first step could offer a big payoff, it's far more likely to leave you right back where you started.

When this happens, we often blame our failure on a lack of motivation, but that isn't really how motivation works. Motivation doesn't inspire us to change habits; small, consistent action fuels motivation. In the same way riding a bike gets easier once you get into a rhythm of small, consistent peddling, motivation increases with each small step towards health.

Small steps, then, provide the consistent action that creates what we call motivation, and that forward motion allows us to create life-long, life-changing habits in the same way peddling can get us across an entire city. This isn't simply anecdotal; it's backed up by the research. Behavior scientist BJ Fogg has laid out the basics for developing new habits through taking small steps that all obey the ABCs:

- **A**nchor Moment: Develop a circumstance that prompts you to do an activity, such as right after you wake up or right after work.
- New Tiny **B**ehavior: Start with the simplest version of the activity so you have no excuse not to do it—like working on flossing by committing to flossing one tooth a day.
- Instant **C**elebration: Immediately after you've done your simple behavior, throw your hands up in the air like you've won the Super Bowl. That triggers a dopamine release in your brain and makes you feel great. And that, in turn,

makes it that much more likely you'll want to do it the next day.

Adapting Fogg's ABCs to small steps towards better health habits is as simple as focusing on five separate small tasks.

- **Take an honest account.** As Dan Sullivan, the founder of Strategic Coach, says, "All progress starts by telling the truth." This should be a regular taking stock of yourself that you can anchor to a specific act in your day (perhaps after you brush teeth in the evening). You can then introduce a tiny behavior like brainstorming and jotting down thoughts on where you are and where you want to be. Afterward, you can do a little dance and celebrate your small success. At root, you are trying to get a clear picture of where you are, truly, in terms of your physical health, diet, and sleep. For instance, do you have a problem overeating? Are you overweight or obese? Do you have lingering health issues you should address immediately? Do you have an issue with alcohol or drugs? To really dig into these answers, you could keep track of your jottings in a journal so you can record progress. You can also speak with trusted friends and family for outside perspective and to make sure your account is truly honest. Record their thoughts as well.
- **Move more.** With your deepest health needs understood, focus next on movement over the "workout" you might otherwise avoid. Instead of joining an intense exercise program, set smaller, more achievable goals in your movement, and anchor that movement to a particular time of day. Then celebrate! When I started out, my movement program lasted only two minutes. Every morning, right

after I got up, I'd do a few pushups and a few sit-ups. Just doing that little bit gave me a real sense of accomplishment. It was also very hard to make a compelling case to skip my two minutes, even when I didn't feel like it.

- **Upgrade one meal.** No need to start by overhauling your whole diet. I started with the meal you feel you can most easily adjust to be healthier. For me, it was breakfast. Fortunately, meals are usually already pretty anchored in our day. Whenever you would normally have that meal, introduce that small behavioral change. Again, this doesn't have to be an overwhelming adjustment. And, if you find a substitute you really love, it can even be your celebration. When I was burned out, I used to eat a bagel with iced coffee at Dunkin' Donuts on my way into work every morning. As I took control of my health, I cut out the bagels (though not iced coffee, I still love that) and started making breakfast smoothies. It turns out, I love smoothies! This became the center of my big celebration for my movement. It was something to look forward to and that helped motivate me as my workouts lengthened. Whether you love healthier food or not, making that small change isn't too burdensome upfront.

- **Moderate everything.** Let's talk a bit more about celebrations. There's a lot of leeway on this, but one reward you don't want to offer yourself is alcohol or another substance. By this time, I'd already quit drinking, so this wasn't a problem for my program, but if you do drink or indulge in other substances, now is a good time to cut down. This goes for other aspects of your life as well, including working and working out. Even if you don't feel you have a problem in any of these areas, it's still worth cutting back on substances or practices that may be affecting your mood.

If you struggle to moderate, that may be a sign that the habit requires more significant and immediate attention.

- **Set a bedtime and wake-up time.** Sleep is the lowest hanging fruit to enhance our performance. It's also a driver of our mood and energy levels. If we want to power these small changes, we've got to get enough shut-eye. And luckily, it's already essentially an anchor point in our day. All we have to do is introduce a tiny behavior to shift those anchors slightly. You can trigger a better sleep schedule by setting an alarm to prepare for bed thirty minutes before sleep, change into your pj's at a set time, or brush teeth five minutes before bed. When you wake up with a full night's sleep, celebrate. Ideally, set a bedtime that works with your schedule and natural rhythms. In particular, focus on when your circadian rhythm naturally wakes you up and plan backwards from there. If your work requires you to get up earlier than you would naturally wake or go to bed later, plan around that inconvenience to still ensure as much good sleep as possible.

The benefit of taking these little steps is that they get you points on the board and some very early quick wins. As every entrepreneur knows, achieving quick wins helps you build momentum on any project. These minor changes can have immediate, noticeable benefits. Very early on, you will start feeling a little better, and you'll have a reason to feel good about yourself. After just a couple weeks, I felt physically healthier and mentally stronger. I also felt proud of myself— an emotion that I had assumed I'd never feel again.

That sense of pride and early accomplishment will do more to keep you pursuing healthier living. Your body will start craving that dopamine rush after you finish moving, and as you feel healthier, you'll naturally want to expand these actions little by little. I certainly found my own movement time increasing in length and intensity naturally. What started as a couple minutes quickly expanded as I became eager to take on new challenges. Over time, I started looking for online programs and bought equipment. At an internet marketing conference, I met Vince Del Monte, whose twenty-minute warmup described in his book *No-Nonsense Muscle Building* became an early cornerstone of my exercise program. I've come to a point now in which I have multiple programs and machines available so I can get some movement in, no matter the constraints of my schedule. If I can only grab fifteen minutes, I can work with that. If I have an hour, my programs can expand into that time.

Similarly, simply by changing my breakfast meal, I found myself naturally expanding my healthy food choices into the rest of my eating habits. When I'd go shopping for ingredients for my smoothies, I'd also pick up healthy food options for lunch. Then, I started buying healthy snacks to keep at the office so I would never feel the need to run out and get fast food. Eventually, I developed a whole routine around these activities, shopping for everything on Saturday, cooking up meals for the whole week on Sunday, and washing up after myself that evening.

Even my bedtime–wake-up time has been able to adapt to my schedule. While I have remained focused on getting the seven-to-eight hours I need, I can adjust my sleeping hours around my schedule so I can get rest and still get everything done.

At this point, I live what most would consider a pretty healthy lifestyle. I'm relatively physically fit, better rested, and fueled by nutritious meals all week. This was attainable not through grand schemes or expensive programs. It was possible simply by taking a few small steps and then continuing on the path I'd started on.

DON'T BREAK THE CHAIN

Crucial to the small-step system is continuation. Remember, motivation is like riding a bike: You have to keep pedaling. This is not unique to healthier living; it's true of any habit. For instance, in order to maintain his motivation to work on his comedy, Jerry Seinfeld has developed a rule he calls "don't break the chain." The rule works like this: Every day that Seinfeld works on his craft, he puts a red "x" on the big calendar on his wall. On that wall, he's laid out the entire year, month after month taped up in front of him. Over the long months of the year, that practice creates a wall of red marks that displays his dedication in a single, unbroken chain of "x"s. Whenever he doesn't feel like sitting down and doing the work, all he has to do is look at the calendar. Because he doesn't want to break the streak, he has motivation to get back to being funny.

I'd imagine someone as wealthy and successful as Seinfeld, a true pro and master of his craft, needs significant motivation to keep the effort up. After all, what does he have left to prove? It's amazing, then, how well a rule like "don't break the chain" works once you've started a habit.

I've found the same to be true for my own habits. In 2015, after listening to a podcast with cold shower enthusiast "Iceman"

Wim Hof, I started taking cold showers in the morning. At first, I was just curious to try it. Hof has made many claims about the value of exposing the body to cold, and I was eager to see if those held up. More than anything, though, I was impressed by how happy he sounded. He was one of the most upbeat individuals I had ever heard. If a cold shower could make someone that joyful, I was willing to suffer the shivers every morning.

And suffer I would. I hate cold water. I am probably the last person you'd assume would be willing to get in a cold shower once, let alone every day. Yet, because of that same "don't break the chain" logic that motivates Seinfeld, I've been taking a cold shower every day since 2015. At first, I figured I'd do it for a few days. But once I got started, I never had a good enough reason to stop. After a couple months, it started to feel like I should have the shower just to keep the streak going.

I'm still taking them now. And every morning I still have to make an active choice: today, I won't break the chain.

THE BEST INVESTMENT YOU CAN MAKE

It's important to keep a healthy streak going, even when it's inconvenient. That's why Rafael has been willing to sacrifice some potential clients. It isn't that he cares any less about his hedge fund; he simply cares more about his health.

And I have to agree with him on that. If you take one lesson from this book, it should be to prioritize the Health Rules laid out in this and the next chapter. The other Happiness Rules provide the keys to creating and maintaining happiness, but these changes can potentially save your life. With just a little more attention paid to your physical health, you'll feel better for longer. You'll have more health and more time ahead of you.

And all the better if you can fill that time with happiness.

THE GIST

There is no real secret to building a good foundation for wellbeing and happiness. It has to start with your physical and mental health. Any system that ignores health is bound to eventually fail.

To start improving your physical health, go for the low-hanging fruit first. Those are the things you can change quickly and a little at a time: eat better, move more, and focus on sleep.

To develop new habits, use BJ Fogg's ABCs:

- Anchor: Anchor the new habit to something you do every day.
- Behavior: Start the habit with something almost ridiculously easy and then build on that as the habit gets ingrained.
- Celebrate: Celebrate the wins, give yourself a high five, pump your fist, and shout out "DONE!" This gives you a dopamine reward and encourages your body to want more.

GETTING YOUR MIND
INTO SHAPE

"The happiness of your life depends upon the quality of your thoughts."
—MARCUS AURELIUS, *MEDITATIONS*,
JEREMY COLLIER TRANSLATION

Early on in my efforts to pull myself out of burnout, I started to ask myself a very fundamental question: Why had I become so negative? It wasn't my diet that had left me feeling isolated and trapped, after all. And a few pushups weren't going to change how cynical I'd become. As I began to search internally, I realized that the negative turn of my everyday thoughts had become so constant, I hardly noticed the process that led me to that pessimism. I had simply come to accept that my thoughts about the hopelessness of my circumstances were absolutely and incontestably true.

I would have to work forever. There were no ways out. I had no savings and no retirement fund, and I never would. This is why suicide had made a certain kind of sense in my darkest moments.

I saw it as an ultimate solution in the case that life truly became intolerable. It seemed, at the time, extremely reasonable.

Why was my default assumption about my life so bleak? After all, I was successful, and I had the means to make money. Even if my relationships needed work, I still had friends and family. I had experienced happiness many times in my life. I had the resources available to me to return to that sense of happiness at some point. So why couldn't I conceive of this moment as a brief setback? Why were my thoughts so concentrated on only negative possible outcomes?

Magdalena had managed to be grateful and happy, even though she was facing a terminal illness. Were my circumstances so much worse and so much more immutable that I couldn't be as happy as she was—*ever*?

I realized that couldn't be right. That meant something in *how* I thought about my life was wrong.

FIRST THINGS FIRST

My issues with negative thinking were compounded by burnout, but it wasn't the only source. My negative thinking predated my burnout, and if I wanted to overcome burnout, I'd have to work on adjusting that thinking first. For me, these thoughts could be dealt with using the tactics in this chapter, but it's important to mention here that there are other sources of negative thinking that may require more extensive professional help. Before we jump into the process of overcoming negative thoughts, I want to reiterate here that this book isn't offering treatment for any psychiatric illnesses you might have. Clinical depression, anxiety, and psychological trauma may include negative ideation, but the root causes of those thoughts run much deeper than the issues we'll discuss here. And overcoming those psychological disorders and traumas isn't as simple as correcting some negative thinking.

If your burnout is fueled by these deeper psychological difficulties, the first thing you need to do is put down this book and find a therapist. Attending to your psychological needs should be your first priority.

Once you have a therapist and you are in treatment, the good news is that you can still pursue the Happiness Rules. There's nothing in this book that should interfere with any recommendations for treatment. However, you can't follow these rules without first beginning treatment. If you want the benefits of this process, you need to be dealing with your psychological health at the same time.

CUT OUT THE NEGATIVITY

It doesn't take a serious psychological illness to lead our brains into a cycle of negative thinking. Our brains are primed to think according to the ideas that we're exposing it to. This is a well-documented psychological phenomenon. In one study by B. S. Wegner, A. M. Hartmann, and C. R. Geist that appeared in *Psychology Reports* in June 2000, one group of female volunteers were briefly shown a picture of a thin model, while the control group was shown a different photo. Those shown the image of the skinny model registered significantly higher rates of general self-consciousness and body self-consciousness than the other group.

Another example comes from Robert Cialdini, in his book *Pre-Suasion*. There, he discusses a study superficially built around people buying furniture online. The study was by Naomi Mandel and Eric J. Johnson and was first published in the *Journal of Consumer Reports* in September 2002. In it, participants were split into two groups. Both groups briefly saw an opening image on a landing page before clicking on a particular furniture page. For the first group, that image was of coins; the other group saw clouds. After they finished shopping, each person was asked the same question: What is more important to you when buying furniture, value or comfort? Overwhelmingly, those who saw clouds said comfort and those who saw coins said *value*.

That's how powerful suggestion is to our minds. Those overwhelming results required exposure for only a couple seconds—imagine how much influence the various screens in your life have over you when you stare at them all day.

As I faced my own cynical thoughts, I began to seek out the influence that may have contributed to my mind taking a negative turn. Exhaustion and stress clearly were playing a part, but I couldn't change those immediately. What I could do was find that outside suggestive force that was augmenting that negativity.

The answer was surprising: sports.

I love sports. I've always been drawn to stories of human excellence. Yet, as I considered my relationship to this form of entertainment, I realized that those stories of excellence were surprisingly rare in my sports consumption. My normal morning routine included listening to a sports radio show on the way to work. It was the first thing entering my mind in the morning, pumping in signals that were priming my brain with a framework that would influence the rest of my day.

For a long time, I assumed this practice was good for me. After all, what better way to start the day than by listening to a subject I so intensely enjoyed? As I listened to it more attentively, though, I found that far from celebrating the triumph of the human spirit and physical prowess, the show focused almost exclusively on drama. Every day, I was filling my mind with criticism, negativity, and gossip. Who said what to whom, who was unhappy on their team and trying to force a trade, who was caught doing something they shouldn't...

It wasn't like this when I first started following sports. When I was younger, sports coverage consisted almost exclusively of broadcasting the games themselves, plus highlights on the evening news and recaps in the paper. Transfer sagas and locker room bust-ups got very little coverage.

As sports media has expanded to fill the twenty-four-hour news cycle, though, those hours have to be filled with something, so sports has become a soap opera, filled with heroes and villains and unexpected twists. It makes for gripping coverage, but not for particularly healthy consumption. I continued to turn the dial for inspiration, but all I was getting was negativity. And when you're burned out, filling your head with that negative gossip every morning can provide all the *inspiration* your brain needs to dwell on negativity for the rest of your waking hours.

WHAT'S GOING INTO YOUR BRAIN?

Sports is by no means unique in its increase in drama and coverage. What is unique is this era in which we place our brains under 24/7 stress. We're inundated with mental junk food in a way no one has ever been before. There's the 24/7 newsfeed that tries to get your attention by feeding you negative stories about recent events with the most dramatic slant possible. Because fear motivates your attention, every story has to be framed as a crisis. The days of thirty minutes of news in the evening are gone. News is competing for your eyeballs for every second you are awake, and our brains are extremely susceptible to the strategies they use to pull us in.

This is all on top of the standard brain stress that people have been under for generations. My main issue was with talk radio, after all, a form of media that's been around for more than a century. And there's still the lingering issues with habits of bringing work home instead of leaving it in the office or allowing ourselves to be subsumed by office gossip.

All of that would be trouble enough, but these days, we have even more to deal with, thanks to social media competing for our attention. This is even worse than cable news because social media companies have developed algorithms that calculate exactly how much drama you need to keep you staring at their site. They know what you're interested in, and they will keep delivering your drug of choice to you forever.

Even if we escape these forces, we still have the ever-present, ever-pleasant resource of streaming on demand. I have nothing against Netflix and HBO—there's plenty of great programming on both—but in some ways, that makes streaming the most insidious of the forces competing for your brain space. Many of us are aware that cable news and social media can have a negative effect on our mental health, but what about *The Office* or those cat videos on YouTube? Aren't those making us feel better?

Sometimes.

Watching an episode of a great show can be great fun and mentally healthy. However, most people aren't putting on a single episode of prestige television every evening and discussing it over tea with their spouse afterward. Instead, they're binge watching—and have you ever heard of binging being used in a healthy fashion?

Having unending, high-quality (and low-quality) television at our fingertips is not necessarily better for our brains than skimming social media for hours. The only difference is that you are using a higher-quality drug. Your brain is taking in that television the same way it takes in social media. It pacifies your mind with every moment of humor or drama. And at the same time, it's turning off from your problems and leaving you disengaged from your life.

In small quantities, this is great. I love TV just like everyone else. But when it becomes the center point of your evening, it's taking away all the time you might have spent reinforcing a human connection, working out, or learning about something that really interests you. In this sense, it's exhausting you as much as it's providing respite from your troubles.

BE MORE SELECTIVE WITH YOUR BRAIN SPACE

What's the solution here? One option would be to go cold turkey. Close your social media accounts. Cancel your cable and streaming subscriptions. Start getting the local paper for your news. And simply live without all of this negative influence on your brain.

For some, that may be required. However, for most of us, the point is to be selective in how we handle these influences. Think of it like drinking. If you enjoy having a drink and you can drink responsibly, by all means, have a drink. Just don't drink a six-pack every evening after work. If you want to enjoy a show, it brings you joy, and it isn't what takes up hours of your time every evening—go and watch. The point is to achieve a healthy balance and to give your brain time to recover from the constant stream of information flowing into it.

"It's not what happens to you, but how you react to it that matters."

—EPICTETUS

To reach this equilibrium, we have to be mindful about our current consumption and our ideal consumption. Look at your media diet today. How much of it is actually necessary? How much of it provides you with genuine happiness? How much of it makes you feel worse? How much of it makes you feel like you're inadequate or leans into your fears and biases?

When you consider adding to your media diet, ask yourself how it will improve your mental health. Is it challenging your curiosity or creativity? Are you learning something from it? And is there anything else you'd rather do than take in that content? Remember, the time you spend on a show or on

Facebook could be spent meeting people, meditating, reading, or working out. Is this content worth your time?

The answers to all these questions will be different for different people. For some, there's great value in a little time on Instagram. For others, it's better to cancel the account or set a time once a month to check in. Some people do feel happier after watching *The Great British Baking Show* or *Ted Lasso*. Others were only turning it on to pass the time.

The point here isn't to tell you how much or what you should watch, only that you should think hard about how you approach your media consumption. Putting the TV on every evening or sports radio on every morning is a choice. Make sure it's the right one for you.

AUTOMATIC THOUGHTS

Even with the healthiest diet for our brain, we are still going to encounter negative thoughts. This is inevitable because we are not in charge of our automatic thoughts in the same way we are for our more directed thoughts. I can choose to think about my favorite vacation, but I have no control over the random thoughts that pop up in my mind throughout the day. In this respect, our thoughts think themselves, as many meditative traditions will tell you.

The upside to this lack of control is that you aren't at fault for having negative thoughts. When you're facing burnout, your automatic thoughts often turn negative—even without the help of Twitter. However, this doesn't mean you have to surrender to these thoughts. Recognize that you have a choice: whether you want to dwell and ruminate upon these automatic negative thoughts or not.

We often forget we have this option. Instead of questioning these thoughts, we believe them as automatically as they were generated. We believe them so intensely that we end up arguing for our own limitations—to the point that we challenge those who present us with a more positive interpretation of ourselves or our circumstances.

I see this all the time. Recently, I was speaking to a coaching client. He told me about all his problems and even predicted his future. He didn't make enough money. He was unhappy in his work. His friends drank too much. His kids were moving out, and once they finished college, they'd leave him behind. And at that point, there wouldn't be enough savings left over for a decent retirement. He would be trapped in this moment of misery for life.

This person was projecting their life forward for decades and couldn't see any possible improvement. When I suggested that there may yet be unseen opportunities to change his circumstances and that, regardless, there must be some things in his life that would give him joy, he told me that wasn't true at all. There was simply nothing but disappointment ahead.

Reading that description, it probably sounds ridiculous to you, but when you're trapped in that burnout mindset, you aren't thinking rationally—and you aren't open to outside perspectives. It is pessimism all the way down.

It doesn't have to be this way. There is a way to move past

those thoughts and think other thoughts. And it starts with putting up blinders.

PUTTING UP YOUR BLINDERS

While we have no choice over what automatic thoughts appear in our minds, we do have a choice whether we are going to identify with a thought and follow it down a chain of thinking—or if we simply let it pass into oblivion. Essentially, we can put up blinders to our negative thoughts. We've all seen horses on the street wearing those flaps of plastic on the sides of their heads. They have these so they won't be distracted or become anxious by what is happening around them. It doesn't make those things go away, but they don't interfere with the horse's behavior. We can do the same with our negative thoughts. We can't stop those negative thoughts occurring, but we can turn a blind eye to them.

Let me give you an example of how this works. I regularly send emails out to people interested in learning more about coaching. Many of the people who sign up for this are current or former patients of mine. Normally, I BCC that list so that no one can see anyone else's email address. On one occasion, though, I accidentally CC'ed everyone, allowing every recipient to see everyone else's email.

Now, I should not have shared those emails, but it was an accident. And of the whole list, only one person was upset. However, the thought that first jumped into my mind after this happened was, "I suck. I shouldn't try to do my own marketing. I don't have what it takes to do sales and coaching. This would not have happened if I just stayed in my lane. I should quit." In that moment, I was filled with shame. It would have been easy to really give myself a hard time over that mistake. Instead of indulging that thought, though, I decided to dismiss it and give myself a break. I put up blinders against my natural instinct to self-flagellate and choose to focus on the fact that anyone could have made that mistake. I didn't have to ruin my day thinking about it.

It's part of the human condition for our thoughts to sometimes assume the worst of us or our situation. If you get a call from a big customer, your automatic negative thoughts sometimes suggest it's terrible news. They want to complain. They want a refund. They're leaving you for a competitor. You don't have to indulge those automatic worries, though. You can simply refuse to think about them and wait to find out why your customer is calling.

In AA, there's a slogan: "Think, think, think." This isn't pointless repetition, it's recognition of the control we can have over our thoughts, grounded in Cognitive Behavioral Therapy. It works like this:

- The first "think" is your automatic negative thought that you have zero control over. This is when the customer calls and you automatically think they're mad.
- The second "think" is when you interject intentionally in the process. At this moment, you choose to examine the first thought. Is that true? Is it possible the customer is calling for another reason?
- The third "think" is what you choose to think after that examination. Whether the first thought was true or not, you can choose how to feel about that thought. You can

choose to think "if something's wrong, we'll fix it. And maybe he's very happy with the product!"

In essence, you can't keep your thoughts from thinking themselves, but you have control over how much you focus on those thoughts if you are mindful about where your mind is drifting. When you have one of those negative first thoughts, there's no need to feel bad about either the thought or the fact you're having it. Instead, focus not on that thought or trying to stop it but on thinking up a second thought faster.

If this sounds like a basic principle of meditation, it is. Although I came to this practice through the theories underpinning cognitive therapy, meditators have been putting up blinders for thousands of years. One of the keys of meditation is recognizing a thought but avoiding getting lost in it. It's a practice of observing thoughts. When you do lose yourself in thought—when your thoughts start thinking themselves—you bring yourself back to focusing on your breathing. If putting up blinders is difficult for you, I recommend you consider taking up the practice.

The power of blinders is not in removing negative thoughts from your life but in allowing you to avoid constantly dwelling on negative thoughts. You can't stop the thought that you're a failure or nothing will ever improve from entering your mind, but it's your choice whether you wallow in that thought and ruin your day or ignore it and keep making progress.

GIVE YOURSELF A BREAK

There's one final key to improving your mental outlook before we move into our next set of rules, and that's simply taking some time to clear your head. In Chapter 3, I said that vacations won't solve your burnout. That is true, but that doesn't mean you shouldn't take one. If you can, get some time away from the pressures of work and everyday stressors. This won't change the foundational habits or perspectives that led you to burnout, but it can offer you some respite and a chance to regain some energy to invest in the rest of the Happiness Rules process.

The key here is to recognize what a vacation can and cannot do for you. Many look at vacations the same way they see crash diets. In other words, they mistake a short-term improvement for a long-term fix. And just like a diet, if you expect long-term improvement from a vacation, you're likely to end up at least as mentally and physically exhausted as you were when you left. If you see it as a chance to recover enough to make more significant changes, it can be extremely valuable.

Whether you can take an extended break or not, it's also worthwhile to reorganize your schedule to create pockets where you can recharge and focus on improving your happiness. You may assume this is impossible because of the importance of your position, but there are ways to make this adjustment.

The author Cyril Northcote Parkinson coined what is now called "Parkinson's Law," which states, "Work expands so as to fill the time available for its completion." In other words, if you leave your time open to meet your obligations, those obligations will eat all your time. Alternatively, if you set tight deadlines for your work in order to give yourself a little extra time, you will meet those deadlines—because you have to. Time is a great motivator.

So if you give yourself until five to finish a project, your mind will automatically focus your resources to get it done by that time. If you give yourself until eight, your efforts will expand to fit that timeframe—or else fill the remaining hours with another project.

At the same time, we can build in intentional recovery time into our days. Between tasks or every few hours, we often take breaks. For a few minutes, we go on Twitter, Facebook, or Instagram and scroll for a bit. But those five to ten minutes we take three or four times a day are better used as intentional recovery time. We can go for a walk, stretch, do some jumping jacks, meditate, or concentrate on our breathing instead of numbing ourselves until the time is up.

This is a particularly important lesson for entrepreneurs. Most workers are not in charge of the time limits set on their efforts. A project due date is set for them, as are their hours of work. They have three weeks for a project. They start each day at eight and finish at five. The time is set. Each day, they get done what they get done, and they arrange their time and energy to achieve what they need to within those limits.

But no one sets those limits for the head of the company, unless the boss sets it for themselves. And far too often, entrepreneurs fail to create their own constraints. That means work never ends. There's never a time when work isn't happening.

And if work is always happening, there's never time to take care of yourself. We have to break this cycle if we want to pull ourselves out of burnout. You have to set rules and hold yourself accountable to them. Only you can put the railing up to keep you from driving over the edge. You have to be the one to give yourself a break—and to stick to it.

EMBRACING A SENSE OF CONTROL

When I realized that sports radio was framing my day negatively, I replaced it with podcasts. Instead of hearing about the drama surrounding superstar athletes, my morning thoughts focused on learning about new things that I found interesting. That simple act of learning about topics that engaged my curiosity added an immense amount of pleasure and energy to my day.

Combined with my new focus on my physical health, it undeniably increased my level of happiness.

After just a few weeks, I found that I spent less time brooding over my limitations and more time thinking outside the box again. Feeling healthier and more energetic thanks to my focus on movement, I suddenly felt like pursuing some of the ideas I was hearing about on those podcasts. Why couldn't I start implementing the business strategies of those hosts and interviewees?

The more I thought about it, the more realistic such opportunities seemed.

At the same time, I felt a noticeable increase in the sense I had control over my life. I may not have been able to remove the financial pressure at the root of my stress, but I could choose to engage in an activity that made me happier. So I wasn't quite as trapped as I thought I was.

In fact, in place of those negative thoughts, I found a new feeling to concentrate on: gratitude. Much research has been done on the value of gratitude to prime the brain in a positive direction. In one interesting study conducted by Kennon M. Sheldon and Sonja Lyubomirsky that appeared in *The Journal of Positive Psychology* in 2006, gratitude and visualization of the Best Possible Self were studied and showed positive results in increasing happiness scores.

The article reviews ways we can prime for success by imagining a future in which the work is done and everything has gone "the best possible way that things might turn out in your life." This primes the mind "in order to help guide your decisions now."

Achieving this positive mindset may not happen overnight, and it does not require immediate, major changes. A lot of the changes in the Health Rules are not huge. No one expects you to start training for a marathon overnight or turn off the TV every evening and start reading *Ulysses*. But by making these small changes, you can demonstrate to yourself that you are still in control of your life. You can still make choices for yourself, and you can still get out of these circumstances—even if you have to do it one small step at a time.

And that is the perfect mindset with which to approach the rules on growing into happiness.

THE GIST

As with your physical health, you can start improving your mental health by reaching for that low-hanging fruit.

Cut out negativity in your environment from sources like news media, social media, and people. Our brains are remarkably easy to "prime" with even brief exposure to negativity, so limit the negative as much as possible.

You can also stop indulging "automatic negative thoughts" by putting up blinders to them rather than wallowing in them. You can start to do this through the "think, think, think" process developed in AA.

Finally, set rules for when to stop working. You won't always be able to follow them, but creating clear boundaries to avoid "workaholic" working is important.

By making these small changes, you can start to reorient toward a sense you are in control and even "prime" the mind for greater happiness and opportunity.

PART III

THE GROWTH
RULES

LEARN AND GROW

"I am always doing that which I cannot do, in order that I may learn how to do it."

—VINCENT VAN GOGH

Reflecting upon my period of burnout after I made my way back to happiness, I stumbled upon a curious cause of my previous trouble: aside from being overworked and overstressed, I was simply too good at my job. I realized this early on in my coaching career. As I was helping others explore ideas and opportunities, I realized that one of the reasons I had fallen into my own rut was because I had stopped being curious about my work in psychiatry.

The problem stemmed from the fact that I already knew how to be a good psychiatrist. I'd done all the studying, and over the decades, I had honed the skills I required to guide my patients back to mental health. I'm not bragging. I'm sure there are better psychiatrists in the world, and there were obviously new discoveries and specialized knowledge I could have explored. However, I had reached a point in my career where I could get through the day without having to challenge myself. I could work on autopilot, and it's hard to feel happy when you're spending your life on autopilot.

It all clicked into place when I stumbled upon a definition of happiness I'd never heard before. In his book *The Happiness Advantage*, Shawn Achor relates an Ancient Greek definition for happiness that remains very fitting today: "the joy we feel striving toward our potential." No wonder I felt trapped before. I had stopped striving, and I had convinced myself that I couldn't fulfill my potential.

To strive once more, I needed new challenges that would force me out of autopilot. It might seem counterintuitive, but what I needed to get over my exhaustion was work that I found challenging—and interesting.

CHALLENGES ARE GOOD

In a busy, stressful life, we often take every chance to make things less challenging. This is why every possible device eventually includes a Wi-Fi feature that allows you to operate it from your phone. Whether it's turning the lights off in the house, turning the heat up on the grill, or changing cycles on the washing machine, people prize having fewer steps in the tasks they have to accomplish every day.

In some ways, this is one of the key motivators in entrepreneurship. Entrepreneurs are always trying to remove friction from the purchasing process for their customers and from their internal processes for their employees. Any time a challenge can be eliminated, we make a point of doing so.

As a business strategy, this is a sound one, but there are limits to how far we can press this instinct in our lives without facing some negative consequences—because it runs against our natural curiosity. Humans are innately curious. Our brains want to explore our environment. And this makes sense. Our species has existed for hundreds of thousands of years, and we were hunters and gatherers for most of our existence. It was only twelve thousand years ago that we settled into sedentary farming societies—not much time at all in evolutionary terms. For the rest of our existence, the drive to wander from the cave and find new potential sources of food or the location of previously unknown dangers was essential.

Now imagine you're one of these early hunter-gatherers and some benevolent god comes down and starts leaving a deer carcass at the mouth of your cave every day so long as you stay within the cave. How long would you remain happy with that state of affairs? True, there would always be food—and food was not something to take for granted back then—and you would have a previously unimaginable level of safety and security. But humans have deeper needs that go beyond our basic necessities. You would still feel the urge to get out, explore, and discover new things. At some point, this blessing would start feeling like a curse. The cave would no longer be a refuge; you would start to feel trapped.

This hypothetical and ahistorical example may seem farfetched, but we have created such caves for ourselves in the modern world. Over the past couple centuries, it has become easier and easier to meet our basic needs. For most of us, food, water, safe shelter, and clothing are readily available and affordable. In fact, we often don't have to leave our caves to acquire these things. They'll come right to our door. It's fairly easy to live a life between two locations: home and the office. And, increasingly, we may be removing offices from that system.

While they may not consider it the case, those who find their work challenging are lucky. Even if we think we don't want the hard projects that push and make us stretch just a bit outside our comfort zone, that struggle quells the need to take on new challenges.

Remember how great it felt the last time you managed to overcome a major problem at work? You did the research, consulted people, came up with a solution, implemented it, and saw fantastic results. In fact, even when the results weren't as great as hoped for, that process was still electrifying—and left room for learning some very important lessons. Such events stick in your mind because they fulfill this particular need we have. That's the same feeling our ancestors would have experienced after climbing into a ravine a few miles from the cave and coming across a mastodon colony or a field full of ripe fruit.

But what happens when these events no longer take place? How do you feed that drive to explore and take on new challenges when there are no more challenges in your work or your personal life?

That crucial satisfaction of your curiosity disappears. And in its place, you feel stifled and unfulfilled, even when things are going well. Essentially, you start to feel burned out.

So if we want to pull ourselves out of burnout, we're going to have to re-engage that curiosity.

GROWING INTO FLOW

Think back to the last time you felt like you were at your very best. What did that feel like? For me, it's that moment when I'm working that everything just seems to click. The answers arrive to problems almost instantaneously. I lose track of time because I'm so engaged in my tasks. Everything just seems to work, and it all happens almost automatically.

We have a name for moments like that: flow. Flow, as a psychological term, refers to the state in which you feel your best and perform your best. You're in the zone, as they say in sports commentary. You're so engrossed in your work, you lose your sense of time and of yourself. You sit down at the desk, and the next time you look up, it's the end of the day. Your progress is significant, and it all feels effortless.

And just as importantly, *you* feel really good.

Flow describes those times when things are just going right. You're hitting all your shots; your ideas are coming out clearly and easily; your decisions are quick and definitive.

We've all felt it, and we'd all like to enter it again. Yet, due to your burnout, it's likely that it's been some time since you were in the flow. Why is it that you can't get back to that state anymore?

It all comes back to that hunter-gatherer drive to explore.

The flow state is hard to access when we are doing what we know well. When we're stuck doing the same thing and never challenging ourselves, instead of flow, we end up on autopilot. Like flow, autopilot is a dissociative state in which we disconnect from our normal experience of reality. However, autopilot disconnects us from the external world—it's all internal thought to the point we miss what's happening. We've all experienced this when driving. We're cruising down the road for fifteen minutes before we realize we can't remember the experience of driving the car. With flow, on the other hand, we lose not the external but the internal focus on ourselves. It's almost like we're outside ourselves, watching as we do something effortlessly. This allows us to do our best work at a rate and quality we are normally not capable of.

Because of those hunter-gatherer instincts, we generally feel that autopilot is useful for boring or repetitive tasks and flow feels good and rewarding. And that's because autopilot comes when we're stuck in our comfort zone, while flow tends to occur when we are just over the edge of that comfort zone where new possibilities occur. There's a time and place for both, of course, but if we become stuck on autopilot, we have to challenge ourselves so our best instincts kick in.

That short distance from our comfort is key. There are limits on how far we can push ourselves, and flow tends to occur when we push ourselves *just a little* beyond our current capabilities. You won't access flow by picking up a musical instrument you've never played before, for instance. Remember, those hunter-gatherers are going a little farther into the wilderness, not running away from the safety of their community entirely.

According to entrepreneur and author Steven Kotler, we can even put a number on how far we should stretch beyond our comfort zone. Kotler calculates it at 4 percent. The ideal circumstance to enter flow, then, would be one in which you are comfortable with the vast majority of the work involved but there's a small element that is new and that intrigues your mind. The size of that gap from your comfort zone is important. If the challenge is too great, you can't get into flow because it's so far beyond what you know and can accomplish now. You have to consciously try to learn the new skill or information. If it's too close to what you already know, there's no stretching yourself and you end up remaining on autopilot.

So if we want to return to happiness, we have to start looking for opportunities in which we can stretch ourselves that 4 percent by learning and growing in ways that satisfy that explorer instinct within us.

HOW TO START LEARNING AND GROWING AGAIN

No matter how good you are at what you do, there's always potential to learn and grow in life. All you have to do is open yourself up to the possibility of new challenges. Those challenges may or may not occur within your traditional responsibilities in the office, but they are present if you seek them out.

I discovered this in my own journey out of burnout largely due to my personal circumstances. I needed more income, and I didn't see how to earn it through my psychiatric practice. The only way I knew to earn more money was through working more, but I was already stretched to my limit. I also didn't know how to immediately improve that practice or my fractured relationships. As far as I could tell, the only option left in that moment was to seek out new opportunities outside my specialization. I'd have to expand if I wanted to overcome these pressures.

Pushing aside the sense that I could change nothing, I began wondering how I could take my psychiatric knowledge and package it in a way that could reach more people. Just thinking about this idea improved my outlook. The very possibility of pursuing this project—perhaps of having a project at all—excited me. Though it may surprise you, I was realizing, for the first time, that I had a lot of freedom as an entrepreneur. I'd never really thought of myself in that way, but once I did, it opened up the reality that I could choose to grow my business and expand my earning potential however I saw fit.

I started to read more and listen to podcasts to gather ideas. During this period of exploration, I came across the book *So Good They Can't Ignore You*, and I was struck by the advice of author Cal Newport, who argued that we can best open ourselves up to new kinds of success by seeking out our "adjacent possibles."

Adjacent possibles are knowledge, skills, and opportunities that are just out of reach. Imagine yourself within a room that seems to have no exits. This is your world in burnout—one in which you are an expert but don't see any escape. You know everything within these four walls, and you are comfortable with everything encompassed within it—but you also feel exhausted and unsatisfied when stuck within these borders. For me, this was the room in which I was a psychiatrist, a father, and a husband. I knew how to do all these things, but I was burned out from the responsibilities and the limits I felt within these walls.

What Newport argues is that you aren't seeing the room clearly. According to him, there's a door on each wall that you can travel through—for a total of four in each room—but I'd take the point further. I think that there are actually doors all around you. More than that, these doors are unlocked, and you can choose to open one at any time. Behind each door, in each adjacent room is a skill, interest, or area of knowledge that is just beyond your current reach. With only a small commitment of resources, time, and energy, you can explore and learn about what is within this room as well. That room also has many doors, and opening a new one leads you a little further still from your initial expertise until you incrementally move into a new world of learning, knowledge, and possibility—one filled with new networks and new capabilities.

Imagine if each room was only about 4 percent outside your comfort zone, allowing you to experience the flow state as you explore interests outside those you encounter every day. It's worth pointing out here that these doors do stick a bit when you first try to open them. There's a natural resistance we feel when trying to challenge ourselves and enter the flow state. Anyone who's ever felt that desire to quit a workout as soon as it gets a little hard knows that sensation, the motivation to quit or delay what doesn't come easily. It's the same reason we delay sitting down to start that novel we've always intended to write or pick up that instrument we want to learn. It's slightly uncomfortable to pull at that door.

This is a sensation everyone has, and we have to be willing to push ourselves through it to reach flow. We have to pull at that door a little to open it because we know there's value in what is on the other side.

This is how I learned my way out of burnout and the stressors at the root of my exhaustion. I needed more income, so I walked through the first door into a series of rooms that covered the process of creating and sharing information products. This area was only a slight stretch for me because the information I intended to sell was based on my knowledge of psychiatry. I decided to find a poorly explained psychological condition and offer more information on it. I settled on bipolar type II—a mental illness that isn't well understood by most people, including professionals. I had all the basic knowledge about that condition, but in order to share it, I would need to stretch myself to create an online program to share that knowledge.

Within the first room, I learned about writing scripts for online videos. One room over, I learned how to upload videos. Another room, and I was learning about video editing. One room further, and it was tracking data on YouTube. Eventually I was running into rooms where I learned principles of online marketing and branding.

Not every room hit that 4 percent mark beyond my comfort. For instance, at one point, I decided I needed a website and spent some time trying to learn how to code. That was way beyond my capabilities at the time. I felt lost and overwhelmed. So I backed out of that room and focused on others that came a little more naturally.

Admittedly, skipping the coding room slowed me down and delayed how quickly I could monetize this project, but even though my second income stream was going to take longer than I'd hoped, I found I wasn't upset by the setback. In fact, at some point in this process of jumping from room to room, the potential for income had become secondary. The primary reason I was pursuing this activity was because I was *enjoying* myself. In fact, I was *happy*. For the first time in months, I found that the hours would fly by when I set about a task. After giving it up as lost forever, I was in the flow of my work.

A project that had started just one room over from the expertise that I found stifling had now taken so much pressure off that I could give myself a longer runway to find a solution to my financial problems. I still had the same obligations and limitations that had led to my burnout, but now, I felt like there were possibilities on the horizon. I could see a way forward.

I've been opening new doors ever since. At some point, I opened a door that showed me a way to help people become their best selves and overcome setbacks like burnout. This was the key to making a bigger contribution to the world that I didn't even know I'd been looking for, and it has set me on a course of engaging challenges for the rest of my life. Ultimately, those doors have led me far beyond psychiatry—all the way to this book.

This is why learning and growing has to ground the next set of rules that help us on our way back to happiness. Learning and growing spurs us back into expanding what we are capable of doing, and along the way, we may just stumble upon the tools we need to build the connections that allow happiness to flourish through community and contribution.

THE GIST

We need challenges. It's hard to be happy being on autopilot.

By nature, we need to be learning. You should seek out the flow state—the state in which we feel our best and perform our best. According to author Steven Kotler, it occurs when we are operating about 4 percent beyond our capabilities, in a "stretch but don't break" situation.

You can also find new interests by cultivating the habit of exploring "adjacent possibles" that relate to your current strengths and interests. These require only a small commitment of time, energy, or money to learn about these new possibles.

Flow and adjacent possibles can lead to a program of learning and growing, all while hunting for new opportunities.

STRENGTHENING CONNECTIONS

"Other people are the best antidote to the downs of life and the single most reliable up."

—MARTIN SELIGMAN

Among the many rooms I've traveled through from burnout to the happiness I feel today, one provided me with a particularly surprising revelation about myself. That room began with the study of marketing. I knew that if I was going to reach a large audience, I needed to learn how to market my ideas. One of the recommendations I came across was to start speaking publicly to my target audience. This would allow for a more direct connection and a chance to hear what they were seeking.

I entered this room with particular trepidation, assuming this would be a necessary but rather painful exercise. I have always considered myself an introvert—someone who is better in one-on-one situations. This was why I was so good with my patients. I felt extremely uncomfortable at the idea of stepping up on a stage and engaging a crowd. It's possible that if I hadn't been so convinced by the value of this project, I may have backed out. But I wanted to get the word out about my program on bipolar type II, so I pushed myself to try it.

I reserved a conference room at a local hotel, and I sent out flyers to local therapists and primary care doctors in the area, advertising my free talk. The plan was to offer some remarks on the illness and then have a Q&A. My expectation was that a few dozen people might show up and they could spread the word about my upcoming online program.

The results did not match the expectation. When I arrived, the room was overflowing. There was so much enthusiasm, I ended up having to turn that single talk into a series of three.

What shocked me more than the reception to my project, though, was how much I enjoyed speaking publicly. It wasn't like the cocktail parties I'd attended with dread. I was invigorated. In fact, I couldn't wait to get back up on the stage again.

What I didn't realize at the time was that this shouldn't have been a surprise at all. Connecting our learning and growth to others is a critical part of establishing a consistent sense of happiness. Public speaking on a topic I was passionate about was so appealing because it hit all four of the big Cs at the heart of happiness built on strong relationships—Connection, Community, Collaboration, Contribution. Simply by sharing what I knew, I was creating connections. Through the talks, I was forming a community with those in the audience. The

Q&A instilled a collaborative environment in which we were all learning together. And that process allowed for a real sense of contribution to others.

It was a perfect recipe for happiness.

THE EVOLUTION OF COMMUNITY

In his book *Sapiens,* Yuval Noah Harari paints a picture of the origins of our species. Two million years ago, there were several species of furry ape-like hominids walking around the planet. None were at the top of their respective food chains, but they were all surviving. Then, 70,000 years ago, an invasive species took over everything: homo sapiens. Everywhere we went, we became the apex predator. We wiped out massive, intimidating species: mammoths, giant sloths, saber-toothed tigers. All of the other hominid species eventually became absorbed into our dominant line. We've been strengthening our control over the planet ever since.

Why us? Why were we the ones to conquer the world and not the larger and previously more successful Neanderthals?

Likely, it was a two-part cognitive revolution 70,000 years ago that gave humanity the advantage we needed. In the first place, humans developed the ability to imagine abstractions outside of themselves. Thanks to this evolutionary development, humans could imagine what didn't exist and attempt to create it. As Harari points out, one of the earliest sculptures we have is of a man with a head of a dog. In that drawing— one a child might make today—a human being had imagined something that had never existed before.

It's true that we weren't alone in this skill. We have limited evidence that Neanderthals could also develop at least some creative art. It may be, then, that the second development proved more decisive. This was the moment we took our new creative powers and harnessed them as a community. Instead of simply painting an object on a wall, humans began to work together to develop complex strategies. We became more than creative individuals, we became a creative, collaborating collective. In the end, we survived, and the Neanderthals didn't.

Cooperation is not limited to humans. Many creatures use it. In fact, we have a term for the power of such collective ability— emergent properties. Think of an ant. One ant on its own has very limited capabilities, but as part of a colony, its abilities can work in concert with others to take over a forest. What humanity was capable of doing unlike any creature before or since was to work as a community to create new objects and implement new ideas that didn't already exist in nature. That was the most powerful force nature had ever seen.

It allowed us to become the most dominant species in history— the first species to have a geological age named after it, the Anthropocene. That evolutionary leap is still with us today. We are driven to share our work and our creative energy with others. So when our society isolates us, the result is inevitable. We become more lonely and far less happy.

LONELINESS IS AN EPIDEMIC

The results of evolution in creativity and collaboration are both obvious and obscure. In the first place, we can see all that humanity has accomplished in a few tens of thousands of years. We have fashioned towns and cities full of buildings that keep cool in the summer and hot in the winter. We have roads, cars, television, iPhones, Uber Eats, and ice cream.

Less obvious but no less significant is the innate need we have to act as social animals. If there were ever any doubt about this, most of us learned just how much we need other people during the pandemic in 2020. This need for community is almost as important as our need for shelter. As people age, the quality that is most highly coordinated with happiness and health is the strength of their connections. At the opposite end of the timeline, children can only thrive through community. We've all heard the story of Mowgli growing up in the jungle without society, but the truth is, if a person grows up away from others, they don't become friends with bears—they lose their ability to connect to other people and a larger society.

We crave connection with us and react to social situations subconsciously. Every time we enter a gathering of people, we ask ourselves, "How do I fit in?" We desire to sort ourselves into organizations, structures, and hierarchies. We are driven to create community and find our way to connect, collaborate, and contribute to it.

So the fact that modern life has left us so divorced from our relationships and communities is immensely difficult for our mental health. Our brains haven't evolved since the world that existed seventy thousand years ago when the vast majority of humans lived in a tight community. While there were always some who would leave their communities for a time—traders, trappers, and so on—most of us stuck together.

As hunter-gatherers, we were driven to explore and seek more flourishing lands, but we explored largely as a unit.

This is why I flourished in an environment in which I could share my learning. I had gone out to explore, and I was delivering my discoveries to my community. There is nothing more naturally fulfilling than that.

Unfortunately, such moments are far rarer these days. In the modern era, our communities are fractured. It wasn't that long ago that kids were allowed to run around their neighborhood because every family was established and everyone knew their neighbors. In seemingly the blink of an eye, the family unit, neighborhood, village, town, and even city has been torn apart. Instead of staying in the communities we grew up in, most people move—not once, but every few years. Instead of working at one company for our whole career, people switch jobs regularly. Even if we remain at the same business, there's a constant switching of teams. We don't know our neighbors like we used to. Our friends live three states away, and our families live three states in the opposite direction.

These isolating trends have only been compounded by the invention of the internet, which has shut us away in our rooms, taking us away from interaction in communal spaces. Increasingly, we spend almost all our time on screens. Work is completed on screens. Friendships are maintained through emails or messaging apps instead of letters and in-person meetings. Even dating has been transferred to the app space.

The problem isn't that the technology is new, it's that we've developed such a need for it. We've become so reliant on technology because the bonds society used to offer have broken down. Before, we dated by meeting the friends of our friends or going to community events or church. Even more traditionally, we had matchmakers. Modern apps succeed because those resources have evaporated. We simply aren't as grounded in our communities as we used to be.

This is not the reality for everyone, of course. My younger sister, Patricia, still lives in the same city she grew up in. When I went to a restaurant with her recently, I was struck by the fact that she knew so many people there. She has a close-knit community in which everyone intends to remain a part for the rest of their lives.

Magdalena also had a strong connection to her community. When she got sick, she was only a few months from receiving all her employment benefits from the university. This was so important to her for so many reasons, including that the university would pay full tuition if her kids attended that school or another with a reciprocating arrangement. This benefit in particular had been such a relief for her, a sense of security that she would never have to worry about how to pay for her kids' college. Now, her children might miss out.

Yet, because of her relationships at work, when Magdalena fell just short of being vested, the university community came to her aid. Many people, including some she didn't even know, donated their hours to her to make up the difference.

But my sisters are very much the exception. The vast majority of people in America aren't having that experience. And this is a particularly significant problem for entrepreneurs. We work long hours. We set up our businesses where they can thrive, not at home. We are the traders and trappers who left the community to go out and make something different. And that makes us particularly vulnerable to losing our community—and particularly in need of building a new one.

MULTIPLE LEVELS OF CONNECTION

How do we reestablish a connection to community? Where do we find it in our busy, isolated lives?

When I talk to entrepreneurs, one of the most common issues that come up is that no one understands them. Unlike entrepreneurs, most people have nine-to-five jobs. They show up, they work the required hours, and they get their paycheck. They have their own stressors and concerns, but they don't really understand the particular pressures that come with entrepreneurship. They don't have to live with the strain that comes with ultimate responsibility for so many people. It is hard to explain the stress that comes with a sense of unending work when so much is placed directly on your shoulders.

Even where understanding is possible, entrepreneurs often prefer not to burden others with their difficulties. It feels inappropriate to complain to those who report to us. Instead, we share the glory of success with others and keep the stress to ourselves.

All of this means that we cannot expect to create real connections through traditional channels like work. Others won't understand, and even if they could, it would be wrong to impose on them.

At the same time, many entrepreneurs in burnout have already seen their established strong connections weakened thanks to the work-before-all-else mantra that led them to this point. It's likely family relationships are at least slightly frayed and old friends may have long ago drifted away. Repairing those relationships is important, but it is quite difficult when you feel you have no emotional resources left.

Under these circumstances, the best option available is often to find and join an established community. There are many wonderful organizations focused on connecting entrepreneurs across the country. With a little searching, you may find a local entrepreneurs group in your area. These organizations are wonderful for entrepreneurs who are at the end of their endurance. It can be incredibly therapeutic to enter a space in which everyone understands your frustrations and anxieties. Such a group can become your tribe—a collection of people who accept, support, and encourage you.

Personally, I found joining such organizations as Strategic Coach and Entrepreneur's Organization extremely effective at giving me that long-missing sense of community and connection. As soon as I made my first dollar as an entrepreneur, I joined both.

Your search for community isn't limited to your work as an entrepreneur, either. If you discover new interests while you're learning and growing, you can join groups that share those interests. If you find out you love woodwork, for instance, join a group in town (or online) for those with the same passion. Such organizations offer a place where you can feel free to talk enthusiastically about this topic for as long as you want. And since none of the members are your employees, you can also potentially open up about your personal and professional struggles as you carve up a nice piece of cedar.

Of course, building those deep connections in which everyone feels safe and trusts one another won't happen at the first meet-up, but it starts you on that path.

Alternatively, you could volunteer for a cause you care about. I've had clients who tell me that they prefer volunteer boards to entrepreneurial boards for the simple reason that anyone who joins a volunteer board wants to be active and interact. It isn't a status symbol; it's a place to do something important.

Whatever group you choose—whether it's a food pantry, a birdwatchers association, or a group for entrepreneurs—the point is you can meet people and build authentic connections that strengthen you when you are at your weakest. These groups feed the soul, and they also provide a structure that allows for your busy schedule. Even if you miss a meeting, it won't break any relationships. People will be happy to see you the next time you can join. And they'll always welcome your contribution—which is almost as important as the connection itself.

THE VALUE OF CONTRIBUTION

Entrepreneurs often feel that they already make a significant contribution to society simply by opening the doors of their business. I don't disagree with this assessment. But as we build new communities, we need to look beyond our business and find new ways to contribute.

Contribution is essential to our sense of connection to community. It allows us to feel important and necessary to our tribe. When we contribute, we feel we belong. In our prehistoric tribes, everyone would have contributed to the health, safety, and well-being of all the members. The elders would share wisdom and tend to children. The young adults would hunt and gather food and protect against dangers. Children would learn the ways of the tribe in order to take over when their time came. Everyone had a role, and that role grounded each individual.

So when we create a new tribe for ourselves, we can further cement our sense of connection to that tribe by contributing to its goals. Not only does this give us a sense of belonging, it gives us the chance to think outside of our own struggles.

This is why contribution is a valuable tool in AA. No one comes to AA to make their life a little better, they come because their life is a mess. They are overwhelmed, struggling, and understandably, wallowing in self-pity. In that space, they can develop tunnel vision in which they only see how hard they have it. The advice they receive from AA is always the same: Go find someone who has it harder than you and help them. That advice is so unchanging because it works so well. The perspective you get from contributing to someone who has it worse is extremely valuable. Suddenly, your own life doesn't seem quite so bad—and things don't seem quite so irreparably broken. If you can make things better for someone who has it worse, you can fix your own life, too.

I experienced the same sense of possibility in my talks on bipolar type II. My initial mindset when scheduling those talks was to take another step towards turning my knowledge into more income. This was an understandable primary motivation under the circumstances, but it was undeniably all about me and my needs. I found, over time, that what really made me happy, though, was focusing intensely on the value of what I was going to share.

To experience that joy, though, we do have to earn it. It's undeniable that contributing requires effort on your part. I'm not discouraging you from donating financially to important causes—please do that as well—but the sort of contribution I'm talking about doesn't involve using your credit card. To get the benefits of contribution in the fight against burnout, you have to *do* something. You have to put your own time and energy into this. By physically doing the work, you become part of a community and you collaborate within that community. Working toward a shared goal with others who share your passion is rewarding—but only if you do the work.

Acts of contribution can take many forms. They can involve everything from sharing knowledge and mentoring to building homes or finding homes for stray dogs.

Of course, when you're suffering from burnout, the thought of adding something else to your to-do list can feel overwhelming. But I can tell you, the benefits far outweigh the outlay of effort here. Instead of seeing this as requiring extra energy, look at it as a redistribution of your resources. You aren't over-investing yourself; you're redistributing your energy in a way that pays you back better than your previous system.

If you've done the work on the Health Rules, you may also

find that you have more time available than you previously thought. Is a Netflix binge giving more back to you than an evening spent at an organization where you could make strong connections, forge a new community, and collaborate on some contribution that would provide you a positive sense of accomplishment?

If not, perhaps it's time to start reorganizing your calendar.

IT'S JUST A PODCAST

I know the idea of jumping off the couch in the evening and going to some meeting probably feels like it's too much for you right now. It certainly felt that way to me. However, just like with the Health Rules, you don't have to start by taking a huge leap into community. It's okay to start small.

My first supportive community, it turned out, was a virtual one. I started following podcasters who cast a bigger vision and offered a novel understanding of my opportunities. I followed those who were creating communities I wanted to be a part of. And those connections made me feel a little less isolated.

Here was a place where I could feel I belonged—a tribe of people who shared my interests and who could help me cultivate the skills I needed to participate and contribute to that community in the future.

It was only after I took that first small step that I could start taking the bigger ones. Perhaps that is the way forward for you too, or perhaps you have connections to family and friends that you feel you can strengthen in your current state of burnout. Or you may have a community you have intended to join and feel now is the moment to commit.

Any of these connections are worthy of pursuing. But you must pursue some of them, and you should do so *intentionally*. Intentional choices are those that you consider deeply and commit to. It's the process of recognizing that you have control and taking it in your actions.

In other words, it's the conscious effort to choose your purpose. And that's the final component of the Happiness Rules: the Purpose Rules that enable you to blaze your own trail intentionally and create a resilient happiness that can survive anything life throws at you.

THE GIST

We require a strong social network in our lives to provide meaning. This can be summarized through the 4 Cs: Connection, Community, Collaboration, Contribution.

Connection: The last fifty years have left us feeling isolated from our "tribe," and entrepreneurs are especially at high risk for this because of the nature of their work. We need to rebuild those broken ties to family and friends because there is a mountain of science that tells us the stronger our connections, the healthier and happier our lives.

Community: This is where we fit in; it's our place in our "tribe."

Collaboration: Humanity has dominated nature because of our ability to create well beyond what an individual can achieve. We crave this in our lives.

Contribution: We also crave a way to make our work matter.

We can use technology as a tool to build the 4 Cs in our lives. Find groups you want to join, seek out collaboration, or find your tribe through podcasts.

PART IV

THE PURPOSE RULES

BLAZE YOUR OWN TRAIL

"Get curious.
Talk to people.
Try stuff.
Tell your story."

—DAVID EVANS AND BILL BURNET

The director of my psychiatric residence program, Dr. John Urbach, asked me a question in my interview for my residency program that has always stuck with me: "How comfortable are you with ambiguity?"

It's an important question for someone training to be a psychiatrist. In most medical disciplines, we've gotten very good at collecting data to make a diagnosis. We can run tests and calculate your blood sugar level or the number of white blood cells running through your system. We can use X-Rays, CT scans, and MRIs. There are still limits to our abilities here, but every day we are getting better at figuring out what is wrong and how to treat it.

In psychiatry, though, it's much less clear what is wrong, and there are far fewer concrete tests to give us a clearer picture. This lack of clarity isn't simply due to the mysterious nature of the mind; it is also because the mind is always changing. As Dr. Urbach put it, "We have to recognize that people are not finished products. We are not diamonds; we are clay that is constantly reshaped."

I clung to that fact as I made my way out of burnout. Despite how I felt, I wasn't frozen in place. I could change, and I wasn't nearly as stuck as I thought I was.

Because we are made of clay, we can always reshape ourselves and our lives. We can always change. In fact, we have to change. It is inevitable. And we have the ability to choose how that change manifests. Far from change being something to fret over, this ability to choose our change is our superpower. We aren't trapped in our circumstances. We will change. And we can have control over what that change looks like.

STOP LIVING BY DEFAULT

The knowledge that things can change is central to the Happiness Rules. It's why I introduced the concept back in Chapter 3. We have to believe—to have hope—in change because we have to change our lives to allow the Happiness Rules to work. But recognizing the power and even the inevitability of change are not the same thing as enacting the changes we want to see. To make those changes, we have to flip the switch from living by default to living by design.

This dichotomy—default or design—has been popularized

by life coaching, and for good reason. It clearly lays out the choices we have in how we approach life. Living by default is, as the word suggests, our autopilot option. When we're in default mode, we're simply allowing life to take us where it chooses. We are passive in the direction events push us—following a well-worn path without introspection.

To a certain extent, default living is inescapable. As we've already seen, our brains are wired to seek out a tribe and to find our place within that community. In finding that place, we are unavoidably shaped by the expectations and demands of that tribe and wider society. Whether it is family, school, friends, or work, we will unconsciously absorb ideas and values that shape our actions. Each group tells us what we must do and sometimes even how we should feel if we want to fit in.

You need to go to college.

You have to have a family and kids.

You need to make a lot of money.

A business must always keep growing.

If you want to be a success, there's no time for rest.

It's likely that the early tribes I belonged to led me directly to my career as a psychiatrist. In my family, it was important to be a professional. I was good at science, and I was told by teachers I'd be a good doctor. It wasn't that I didn't have a say in my career or that I didn't enjoy becoming a psychiatrist or working as one, but I was definitely on a default path toward that outcome.

In truth, I simply didn't examine this pressure very deeply when I was young. That is what is at the root of default living: an unthinking acceptance of the direction set by external forces. We come to see that direction as inevitable, and so we allow others to make these choices for us.

But that direction is not inevitable, nor is default thinking. In fact, we are free to design our own rules, even in business. No matter what the tribes you belong to say, you can choose whether it's important to own a fancy car to prove your status as a successful entrepreneur, or whether you need to live in the best neighborhood in town. You can decide if your happiness requires continued growth in your business or adding a zero to your personal wealth.

You can look at where your community's priorities conflict with your own—and you can choose to design your life around your interests.

This is the essence of living by design. It's the act of being intentional in your choices so that you decide what you truly want instead of drifting along with the current.

This isn't always easy, and in some situations, it isn't always possible. It may be that you are constrained to a growth mindset in the office because you are responsible to investors or a board. However, once you start looking for opportunities to design your life, you'll find plenty of fertile areas where you can start making choices for yourself, no matter what your community wants.

FINDING DIRECTION

The big question looming over a transition to living by design is: What do you actually want from life?

Many of us never really take this question seriously. We never question what we want, and so we absorb our priorities from our various tribes. For many Americans, that means money, property, and power in business.

But if we are going to make mindful, intentional choices, it's time to give this some deeper thought. Let's say that you won the lottery next week and you suddenly found yourself free of financial obligations for the rest of your life. What would you do with your time? Would you keep working the way you do now? Would you work less? Would you work at all?

What would you spend your time learning about? What skills would you focus on developing? How would you challenge yourself?

What about relationships? Which ones would you want to cultivate? Would you get closer to family? Reconnect with friends? Work on your marriage?

What groups, organizations, and communities would you join? Which would you leave? How would you choose to contribute to these various tribes?

These are not easy questions to ask, let alone answer—which is why it's easiest to dismiss them as fanciful. You won't win the lottery next week, so why wonder about how you'd live if you did? But there's great value in this exercise, if only because your answers reveal the direction you would steer your life if you had complete control over it. And once you know that direction, you can use it as your north star. You may not be able to bear straight for it, but you can always correct back towards it.

The answer you discover may not be obvious. For instance, it took significant introspection to realize that I had not chosen to pursue psychiatry on my own. And as I began to blaze my own trail outside that field, it took more self-analysis to work out why I had been good at the work in the first place. What skills had allowed me to achieve success in that field, and how could I use those skills as I moved forward?

What I discovered was that the reason I was a very good psychiatrist was not my innately scientific mind or my extensive knowledge of psychology, nor was it my skill as a diagnostician for mental illness. My true skill resided in my ability to integrate different ideas together and distill them into simple pieces. That's what allowed me to help people understand the stray experiences and feelings that were troubling them. Knowing about this skill has allowed me to direct my life towards utilizing it beyond my psychiatric office. Hence, the Happiness Rules.

Our goal should be to dig into each of these questions through introspection and conversation so we can design our lives to emphasize what brings us happiness, energy, and success and to deemphasize what drains our resources. This isn't a matter of one-time, drastic change, but a continuous act of realignment toward our ultimate goals with every choice we make.

EMBRACE YOUR ABILITY TO CHANGE

It's always scary to take a risk. No one knows that better than an entrepreneur. However, I think it's particularly hard to take a leap into the unknown when you've already proven yourself a success in how you currently organize your life. It's one thing to try something radically new when you have nothing to lose—say, when you've cracked and burned because of an addiction to alcohol. It's another to take a big left turn when you've done extremely well in the lane you're currently in.

Under those circumstances, changing direction is a big demand to place on yourself, but the results can be powerful and extremely rewarding. That was certainly the case for Shawn Askinosie. He was a very successful defense attorney—in fact, he was undefeated in the cases he took to trial. He was in very elite company in the legal world, as one of the only people who had gotten his clients off for capital offenses. Obviously, he was very financially and professionally successful.

And he spent years praying for an opportunity to change the direction his life was heading.

At some point, it occurred to him that he'd like to learn how to make chocolate. From lawyer to Willie Wonka is perhaps the oddest career choice anyone has ever made, and I'm sure plenty of people tried to persuade him to forget it. But the idea stuck. It seemed to suit him. Within a few months of first having the idea, he took a trip down to the Amazon to meet the people who actually grew cacao. From them, he learned how to transform cacao into the chocolate he wanted to sell.

With this new knowledge in hand, he walked away from the law and started a chocolate company.

But it wouldn't be just any chocolate company. Shawn wasn't interested in following in the footsteps of Nestle or anyone else who came before. He wanted to build a whole new system. He decided to work directly with farmers. He's so transparent in these business relationships, that he shares how much his company is making and makes sure to give every farmer he works with a good living wage. He also helps farmers evolve their cultivation process to grow cacao more efficiently and transports and sells their other products in America for free.

The system has been so successful and equitable, he's put Fair Trade to shame and helped start the Direct Trade movement.

Askinosie's chocolate company may not look like the definition of success according to certain communities of entrepreneurs or our society at large. After all, Shawn is certainly not making as much as he was as a lawyer, and he could certainly make more if he were less generous with the farmers who provide him with cacao. His work is less prestigious, and he has probably given up some of the benefits that his wealth and reputation would have offered if he'd stuck with law.

But I challenge you to argue that he isn't a success on his

terms. I've spoken to him personally, and I can attest, he is, for the most part, quite happy. He still has his share of concerns and tough days. He still has some angst that he's working through. But overall, he's happy. And how could he be otherwise? He chose the direction he wanted his life to go and he's followed it every day since.

You are in a position to have that kind of transformational impact. You can choose to make that kind of change. Far from being stuck in your current situation, you can lead a life on your terms. For you, it may not be a new career or a new job. It may be a renewed focus on relationships or prioritizing time off for self-care. It may be focusing on your role in your community or finding a new community.

Whatever it is you need to return to happiness, you can chart a way there through the skills, connections, and interests you already have. The results may not always be immediate, but simply by choosing your own direction, they will be profound.

For me, blazing my own trail has been a twelve-year journey in which I have slowly moved from my psychiatry practice to fully crafting my coaching ideas into the Happiness Rules. Over those twelve years, I have woken up every day with work to do, as I learn and grow, strengthen my connections, and find my way forward on my terms.

I haven't had immediate success, but I wouldn't change any of it. Far from feeling lost and burned out, I'm the happiest I've ever been. I can't wait to get to work. I don't lie in bed trying to motivate myself to get up. The morning can't come soon enough.

A path to that life is open to you. But it's for you to create it and follow it. Remember, your ability to choose is your superpower. You don't have to have all the answers now. You don't need to know what you should do or where you want your life to take you from today onward. All you have to do is to choose to start seeking that life and to center that search in the Happiness Rules. So long as you are progressing in the right direction, you're always one step closer to what you really want from life.

Of course, happiness doesn't guarantee there are no problems or setbacks ahead. You will still have bad days. There will still be disagreements with colleagues and those you love. Money troubles won't disappear just because you feel more content in your work. You can still get tired and frustrated, and you can still experience periods of being overworked, overwhelmed, and underappreciated.

The Happiness Rules can't keep life from happening, but they can help you create a resilient happiness to take on those difficulties on your terms while blazing your trail.

THE GIST

We are never finished products. Our ability to choose what our life is and what it will become is our superpower.

To enable that superpower, though, we have to flip the switch from living by default to living by design.

To start flipping that switch, ask yourself these questions:

- What are you uniquely good at?
- What are you curious about?
- What do you want?
- What do you want to contribute?

CREATING RESILIENT HAPPINESS

"Try in all things to be very glad, very happy, very thankful. It is not to quiet resignation I give My blessings, but to joyful acceptance and anticipation."

—*GOD CALLING* DEVOTIONAL

As Magdalena's illness progressed, it became harder for her to do basic things. She had to give up driving. Later, she struggled to even get out of bed. Facing declining health, pain, and death, no one would have blamed her for becoming depressed or angry or cynical.

But she never became any of those things. I'm sure she had dark thoughts at times—it would be impossible and unnatural to avoid such thoughts entirely under the circumstances. But she never indulged in them. Instead of focusing on her worst fears, she chose to focus on her family. Instead of wringing her hands about how unfair it was, she chose to laugh and smile for as much of her remaining time as possible.

She wasn't divorced from reality. She was aware of the state of her health. She knew that she would miss out on decades she had wanted to spend watching her kids grow up. She knew the pain those she loved would face. In the face of those incontrovertible facts, though, she chose to be happy with all her remaining time.

In my last conversation with her, even as she struggled to remember the names of everyone in the family, her mind was focused on her children. She wanted to make sure they would be okay. Even on that day, I remember her smiling.

It's easy to tell Magdalena's story as a tragedy, but I don't see it that way—because she didn't. Instead, she triumphed over everything that came at her because she never let it take her happiness. To the very end, despite everything, her happiness proved stronger and more resilient than anything life could throw at her.

STRUGGLE ≠ UNHAPPINESS

We live in a society determined to eliminate struggle. In a world in which our basic needs are easy to take care of for most of us and survival is assured—again, for most of us— we now work to reduce discomfort, eliminate friction, and increase convenience. Wherever possible, we concentrate our efforts on distracting thoughts of suffering and struggle with acts of pleasure. This is part of why Netflix is such a phenomenon. Why struggle through an evening mulling over why things haven't gone your way when you can fill your mind with your favorite show until you pass out?

On some level, we assume this must make us happier—after

all, we are smiling and laughing for hours as we stare at a blinking box—but mindlessly disconnecting from our reality fails to really provide happiness precisely because it is misguided. We cannot eliminate our sources of discomfort, unhappiness, and misery. We cannot stop stories like Magdalena's from happening to those we love and to us. This is simply part of human existence. When we fail to address these struggles, we don't remove them, we simply let them fester within.

Instead of pretending hardship doesn't exist, we should recognize that it is inevitable. On a planet with gravity we are going to fall and get hurt; struggle and pain are part of life—every life. Even the most cared-for baby will have moments where they experience hunger, cold, and discomfort. Our response to this reality should be to concentrate our efforts on building a resilient form of happiness that can find energy, optimism, and satisfaction even in our darkest moments. Creating such resilient happiness in our lives isn't easy. If we are living life by default, our reaction is often to allow struggle to overwhelm us. But we do have a choice to live otherwise.

I once had a client, Mac, whose business partner treated him abhorrently. After years of disagreements, Mac and his partner had decided their goals were simply not aligned. They agreed to divide the company equally and to move on. Shortly after that, my client discovered that his partner had been in secret talks with a competitor. The two of them had been hatching a plot to work together to take the best employees and customers from my client.

"We'll ruin your dirtbag partner," the competitor vowed.

This was more than just an awful act of betrayal. Potentially, this partner could cost Mac everything. He might lose the business he loved. He might have to leave entrepreneurship and work for someone else again.

Understandably, Mac was in no mood to be optimistic about his circumstances.

"This is terrible. There's no way out of this."

As he detailed the situation, I noticed a theme developing in how he described every aspect of his predicament.

"The situation is awful."

"Everything is going wrong."

"This is so unfair."

"I'll never get over this."

He was stuck in a mental loop. He viewed every aspect of his life, his current situation, and his future through that one lens. The betrayal became the only story he told about his life.

I don't mean to suggest that Mac should have been pleased with this turn of events—feelings of anger and hurt are all too natural in that situation—but there were other ways to frame his current circumstances. There were other stories he could tell.

As I explained to him, crashing into an obstacle does not necessarily equate to tragedy. In AA, you'll often hear alcoholics call their rock bottom moment the best thing that ever happened to them. They say this because all the future growth they experienced was only possible due to that low moment. From the ultimate bleak sign that there was no future, their time in the gutter can come to seem almost like salvation. There's even a term for this: post-traumatic growth.

Nothing about the facts surrounding that low moment has changed. The events and context are all the same. All that has changed is how that former alcoholic views that moment. When measured by their future internal growth and external improvement, it becomes not the end of a journey but the beginning of one.

And that means we can choose, even in our moments of difficulty, to neither evade nor dwell upon the negative but instead to seek a more positive frame for how we experience it.

"In five years," I told Mac, "the story of this terrible, awful moment could be the start of how you changed your life and started blazing your own trail. This could be your moment to chart a course towards a better life than what you've been living, one with less stress and more reward. And there's no reason you have to wait five years to think that way."

Once he embraced this version of his story, Mac could start making the small changes that would make that story a reality. He could focus on his physical and mental health to strengthen him during the tough times ahead. He could expand his understanding by learning about topics related to his troubles, such as legal principles connected to his situation, strategies and tactics to rebuild his business, and possibly new directions he could take if the business did ultimately fail. He could reach out to friends in the entrepreneurial world who would understand a nasty business divorce and offer assistance where possible. And he could prove that he had the ability to choose the ultimate course of his life. There would be options ahead, even if he couldn't see them yet.

Projecting this kind of positive thinking on his difficulties was more than fantasy. In some ways, it was a more accurate picture of his circumstances. As we dug into his situation, we found that his story of a great business taken from him didn't quite live up to the facts. In a more reflective moment, he revealed that he hadn't been enjoying his work for quite some time. Stress at work hadn't been limited to the friction between himself and his partner. He'd felt stifled and unhappy for quite some time.

So why couldn't this moment of betrayal become an opportunity to refocus on the work that he used to love? When prompted on this point, he realized that it was less the company he cared about than the ability to work with high performance teams.

Could he build a new team with his remaining clients and employees?

Could he expand the business into new areas and attract high-level people?

Could he find a position where he'd be in charge of such a team?

Could he find opportunities to work such teams outside of the office?

Suddenly, it all seemed less bleak than it had. This didn't have to be the end of his career; it could be the moment he rediscovered why he'd followed this career in the first place.

And simply at the prospect of taking on that challenge, Mac seemed happier.

Would he have made changes to his work and life without facing that struggle over his business divorce? I'm not sure. Facing up to difficulty is a necessary component of internal growth. Hans Lehr, a friend of mine and the former Director at Saratoga County Alcohol and Substance Abuse, once said that treating depression has eliminated the room for saints. I don't agree with the forcefulness of that opinion, but it's valuable to recognize that suffering and struggle are a part of being human. And they are necessary if we want to strengthen our happiness muscles.

If we don't allow ourselves to struggle, we can't learn how to return to happiness. It's like trying to develop a six-pack when you aren't willing to get off the couch. If you want to build resilient happiness, you have to put the work in—and that means acknowledging struggle and doing the introspective work to create it.

The struggle Mac is enduring will allow him to reevaluate his priorities. The focus he learns to place on happiness now will help him through future difficulties. Likewise, I'm a happier, more productive professional today in a field where I can contribute far more precisely because I faced my burnout as a psychiatrist directly.

Because you are suffering in this moment, you are reading the Happiness Rules, and the Happiness Rules, in turn, can offer you the means to not only cope with that suffering but to eventually skyrocket beyond your previous baseline with a more robust and sustainable form of happiness. If you do the work.

That won't keep the stress, struggle, and suffering at bay forever. No matter how well organized your life, you will face misfortune, disappointment, and setbacks. Business will fail to grow as expected, relationships will fray, sickness will strike you when you least expect it. Nothing in the Happiness Rules—or any other system for that matter—can spare you from this.

But while the Happiness Rules can't control the events that occur in your life, they can give you control over how you respond to those events—so that struggle no longer leads directly to unhappiness. And you never feel trapped in your circumstances again.

Such resilient happiness will not make the suffering hurt less, but it can allow you to gain from that suffering—so that suffering becomes a valuable part of your experience.

I would never want to remove the suffering I felt when Magdalena died. That suffering was a sign of love. It was a necessary pain. And it led me here.

THE POWER OF THE LAST HUMAN FREEDOM

I know that some hard-nosed entrepreneurs will feel this sort of thinking is pointless. After all, if you've built a career on reducing struggle through improved process or innovation, the idea that we should embrace that struggle instead will feel not just alien but hostile. At the same time, if you have always prided yourself on your ability to transcend struggle and push forward, the idea of slowing down to look for happiness within difficulty can seem absurd.

Far from absurd, though, focusing on building resilient happiness for moments of struggle actually strengthens your ability to be a good entrepreneur—because through that resilience you can remain more productive, more decisive, and more effective without falling back into burnout.

The psychiatrist Viktor Frankl discovered the vast potential for resilient happiness in the worst of all possible contexts: Nazi concentration camps. Over three years in four different camps, Frankl found that those who had developed resilience through some inner sense of purpose or meaning were more likely to survive the horrors they were living through. What's more, he argued that this kind of inner strength was a choice. As he put it in his book *Man's Search for Meaning*, "Everything can be taken from a man but one thing: the last of the human freedoms—to choose one's attitude in any given set of circumstances, to choose one's own way."

Following Frankl's observations, we can see how valuable choosing to develop resilience through a focus on happiness can be to our future as entrepreneurs. If we can seek happiness through struggle, we can avoid the sense we're trapped, even when events begin to overwhelm us.

A patient of mine, Todd, is facing such events right now. He is a young, hardworking apprentice butcher at a local grocery store with dreams of opening his own butcher's shop in the future. As far as talent goes, there's nothing that can stop him from achieving that entrepreneurial dream. Despite his innate aptitude for the work, though, he has not seen his prospects improve because he's allowed external events to control his emotions. When the older butchers don't pull their weight, Todd becomes furious. He screams at his colleagues when the meat cases aren't as pristine as they should be or when the customer service is unacceptably slow.

His troubles have gotten so bad that a couple of months ago, he was close to being fired. It didn't matter that he was the best employee at the store; his colleagues couldn't work with someone with that kind of temper.

When he came to me, he told me he felt desperate. "I wish I could calm down, but I can't! These people are making me so angry!"

Instead of responding immediately, I opened my desk and took out a packet of sticky notes. On the top one, I wrote *peace of mind*.

"You see this?" I asked him. "This is your peace of mind. No one can take this from you unless you give it to them. If you start losing your temper and feel like others are taking your peace of mind, just check your pocket. If this piece of paper is still in your possession, then you can hold onto your peace of mind."

He looked a little dubious, but he took the note with him after our session.

One month later, he was a man transformed. At our next session, he burst into the office, shouting, "I've still got it. It's in my pocket!"

A sticky note might seem a bit silly to you, but it worked because the point is valid. Our peace of mind—and our decisiveness, creativity, and motivations—are ours. They don't belong to others. No one and nothing can take them from us. The government can't take them, family can't take them, your job can't take them—even facing your own mortality can't take them away. They are yours, and only you can *choose* to keep them or give them away.

The Roman emperor and philosopher Marcus Aurelius recognized this. As emperor of the largest empire on Earth, he could do whatever he wanted. If someone annoyed him, he could behead that person, and no one would question him. He had absolute power. Yet, when facing such annoyance, he instead chose to seek inner peace. He wrote in his famous *Meditations*:

> The people I deal with today will be meddling, ungrateful, arrogant, dishonest, jealous and surly. They are like this because they cannot tell good from evil. But I have seen the beauty of good, and the ugliness of evil, and have recognized that the wrongdoer has a nature related to my own—not of the same blood or birth,

but the same mind, and possessing a share of the divine. And so none of them can hurt me.

In other words, Aurelius recognized that it was within his power to choose to maintain his peace. It was his to create and hold.

You will have plenty of opportunities to get your feelings hurt and your noses bent out of shape by life. You are guaranteed to have feelings of sadness, anger, frustration, and grief in the years ahead. Your work will always bring with it stress and setbacks. Still, within your life and in your business, you have the absolute power of emperors over how you respond to the circumstances that lead to these emotions—and where you want those emotions to take you.

EMOTIONAL REGULATION

To be clear, you can take this practice too far. The Happiness Rules are not meant to be an excuse to try to shut yourself off from emotion. Despite my reference to Aurelius above, I am not advocating for stoicism or a life of all observation and no feeling.

It is okay—even necessary—to feel anger and sadness. We should feel remorse, hurt, and grief when appropriate. If you lose a major client, you are allowed to feel upset. If your business partner betrays you, you have a right to feel betrayed. The point is that we do not have to let these feelings—or those who motivate these feelings—dominate the rest of our lives.

Think of this like the difference between weather and climate.

Weather is a short-term, localized phenomenon that lasts a matter of hours or days, while climate is a longer-term pattern of weather. Your emotions are your weather systems, they blow through for hours or days at a time. That's great; experiencing that weather is what it means to be human. What you don't want to do is turn your weather into a climate in which your grouchy evening after a bad call with a client turns into weeks of grouchiness or allow frustration at a setback in product distribution to become a sense of frustration in every aspect of your life.

We should recognize that emotions are valuable, including all the so-called "negative" emotions. But we can feel sorrow, fear, and discomfort without letting those feelings become the center of our minds and color every aspect of our lives. Again, Magdalena is the perfect guide here. Though she was undoubtedly despondent over her illness and overwrought at the thoughts of her children growing up without her, she was still able to find joy in many aspects of her life. It wasn't that she denied herself the right to feel these "negative" emotions; she simply left room for the happiness that remained.

We can feel an emotion without gassing ourselves up on it and letting it overwhelm every aspect of our lives. Many of the people I've mentioned in this book have had wonderful families, physical health, financial success, friends, and plenty of other parts of their lives where they could find happiness and feel grateful. Their burnout made it difficult for them to see where that joy resided.

And as we move forward out of burnout, we have to work hard not to be blinded to those other aspects of our lives again. We may yet experience periods of exhaustion, but we can't let that exhaustion define our lives—either within the moment or into our future.

INTERNAL SUCCESS

As we begin to exit burnout and step back into the world of happiness, it's important to maintain what we have gained through this process. If you've ever gone through physical therapy, you know that you shouldn't stop exercising a healed muscle once it's back to its previous health. You should continue to exercise so you reduce the risk of future injury.

The same is true of happiness. We have to maintain our focus on the Happiness Rules even once we pull clear of our immediate issues. And that means keeping up on the internal work that keeps our happiness strong and resilient. We should continue to prioritize our physical and mental health, pursue opportunities to learn and grow, strengthen those connections, seek ways to contribute, and continue to live by design so we can blaze our own trail forward.

At the same time, we should turn away from the external forces we have used to measure our happiness—the growth in our bank account, the speed at which we scale, the praise we receive for our work—and look instead for our own metrics.

To develop such metrics, we have to ask ourselves some difficult questions.

Who am I really? Am I doing the work to get closer to knowing myself?

What am I doing here? Am I making strides in fulfilling a purpose?

Who do I want to be? Am I continually trying to live like the person I want to become?

Who do I care about? Am I strengthening those relationships?

Where do I belong? Am I contributing to those communities?

These are the sorts of questions we should measure ourselves by. From this perspective, we take a full view of our strengths, shortcomings, needs, and ambitions, and we can measure progress by our own standards and for our own happiness. We can recognize that we are not the best version of ourselves—that we are and always will come up short—and that we can do better.

By the measure of such internal metrics, Magdalena was a great success. I can only hope to be a success on that same scale. As you pull yourself out of burnout through the Happiness Rules, I hope you will join me in becoming your own success—on your terms.

THE GIST

We could all learn from my sister, Magdalena, whose happiness was more resilient than disease, discomfort, and loss. We can be happy through any circumstances—without eliminating our other emotions and experiences.

What's more, we have to develop more resilience in our happiness because pain and struggle are as inevitable as gravity.

The Happiness Rules can't remove difficulties from your life, but they can give you control over how you respond to those difficulties. Struggle does not have to lead to unhappiness, as Magdalena shows us.

We must remember the wisdom of Viktor Frankl: "Everything can be taken from a man but one thing: the last of the human freedoms—to choose one's attitude in any given set of circumstances, to choose one's own way."

You can choose the way of happiness—of health, learning, connecting, and blazing your own trail—through everything life throws at you. That is the power you have over your circumstances, whatever they happen to be.

CONCLUSION

That day when, in the midst of my burnout, I stared at a picture of Magdalena and took inspiration from her story to change my own life, I made a pledge to myself and to her: I was going to commit myself to enjoying the ride, no matter what. That's how Magdalena lived, and it's how I've tried to live ever since.

You can see the results of that commitment in this book. In these pages I have laid out my attempt to systematize and codify the tools I used to overcome and stay clear of burnout— so I could enjoy the ride, no matter what. One of the worst feelings I had in the midst of my own struggle was that I was alone and no one could help me through what I was experiencing. I hope this book has provided you the reassurance that not only have others been where you are but that there is a way through this.

I firmly believe that the best thing you could do for yourself today is to take your first small step towards implementing the ideas you've read about here. And tomorrow, take that next step. That step may be as small as buying healthier snacks or taking a ten-, or five-, or even two-minute walk at the end of your day. It may be turning off Netflix a little earlier in the evening and spending fifteen extra minutes reading about something that interests you—or going to bed fifteen minutes earlier. It could be an email to an old friend or signing up for a group that shares your passions.

Whatever step you choose to take, the most important thing is that you take one each day. Go at your own pace, but keep going.

Unfortunately, that's as much as I can do to help you from the pages of a book. Only you can choose to take up these tools and incorporate them into your life. Even if it doesn't feel like it right now, you can change your life, but you are the only one who can do it.

If you are having trouble taking that first step—or your three hundredth—and if you need more than the words in a book to help guide you that next step forward, I have more resources and tools available on my site ManuelAstruc.com. There, you can also access a community of entrepreneurs who have experienced exactly what you're going through.

Once you've traveled some distance from this dark moment, I hope you'll become a part of that community, share your journey with others, and contribute guidance to those taking their first step. That's the only way we can take on the society-wide plague of burnout and begin to shape a happier, more productive world.

ACKNOWLEDGMENTS

This book—and this life—was a long process that required guidance, support, and input from innumerable individuals. On the nuts and bolts of putting this text together, I want to thank my scribe, Seth Libby. What can I say? You are a true professional, and you carried me over the finish line. This book would not exist without you.

I've had so many teachers over the years, but two stand out. Dr. John Urbach was the director of my residency program at The Medical College of Virginia, Virginia Commonwealth University. He was patient, wise, and courageous, and he oversaw the program that turned out many well-trained psychiatrists. Dr. James Levinson, who was the director of the Consultation-Liaison service, maintained high expectations of himself and others. He exemplifies excellence as a physician and teacher.

To my patients and clients, I was told when I started medical school that my patients would be my teachers, and that has turned out to be 100 percent true.

Melissa, I can't do much without you as my right hand, reading my mind day in and day out.

Before happiness, there was alcoholism, depression, and burnout. I caused a lot of pain to my family. In spite of that, they have been there for me, supported me, and helped keep me going, even as I rejected their help and was the proverbial bull in a china shop.

I want to thank Aba and Abu for their perseverance and showing me how to handle big changes—like moving from Spain to Richmond, Virginia, with five young kids (that would grow to seven). Aba always put the family first and never complained. Abu worked his ass off for the family, a trait I picked up and continue to work on moderating.

To my brothers and sisters, you have carried me and loved me when I could not love myself. Salud, you have the biggest heart of any one I know, and you have been there for me at some of my darkest times. Remember the conversation at Skipjack? Pilar, you continue to be an example of the cardinal virtues for me, though with a lead foot and an intolerance for cold showers. Juan, your patience, humor, and ability to connect with others—and the apparent absence of the Abu gene in your life—is awe inspiring. I wish I had been a better big brother. Rafael, what can I say, your transformation on so many levels is an inspiration and living proof that change is indeed possible. Patricia, I admire your love and passion. You are truly a genius at what you do. Jon, Magdalena said, "Take care of my children." You supported and took care of Magdalena in so many ways over the years. What an amazing group of humans you raised. Your quiet strength and good humor are an inspiration.

For Karen, if I'd known better, I would have done better. I appreciate your generosity in remaining a positive force in my life.

And wow, my children. Stuart, your grit, persistence, and openness to maintain a relationship with me after all that's gone down is very much appreciated. Zach, a scholar, a genius, and fabulous big brother, you are in my thoughts frequently. Ellie, you are one of the hardest workers I know, and you have bloomed into a dedicated professional. Your patients are lucky to have you, and I am lucky to have you in my life after everything I have put you through. Luke, you are always in my heart and truly one of the most brilliant minds I have ever been around. You are a gentleman and a class act. Andrew, you are smart, generous, kind, and the least judgmental person I have ever met. The world needs your philosophy and discourse. And Noah, there are dark nights of the soul, but even with that, you lift people up. The world (and I) need your laugh, your music, and heart.

Marlana, you have been the most important person in my life. I will always love you.

And finally for Magdalena, thank you for showing me how to live and love.

ABOUT THE AUTHOR

MANUEL ASTRUC is the founder of Your Next Act, a coaching program to help high-achieving entrepreneurs find the mental strength to not just survive their ventures, but thrive. When he personally experienced the effects of consciously choosing to embrace happiness in his daily life, he knew he needed to share the knowledge with others.

In addition to his role as the medical director of Saratoga County Alcohol and Substance Abuse Services, Manuel works at his general psychiatry practice to help individuals explore and treat biological roadblocks to success, including ADHD, depression, bipolar disorder, anxiety, and addictions.

CPSIA information can be obtained
at www.ICGtesting.com
Printed in the USA
BVHW040002211022
649664BV00007B/6

9 781544 536286